P9-CLR-309

SALAMANDERS and NEWTS
CO-043S

Plethodon cinereus, *the common red-backed salamander of the eastern United States, is attractive but seldom makes a good pet.*

ENDPAPERS:
Ambystoma mexicanum, the axolotl.

SALAMANDERS AND NEWTS

A COMPLETE INTRODUCTION

In American pet shops one of the most common salamanders sold is the Califor-nia newt, Taricha torosa.

Photography: Dr. Herbert R. Axelrod; G. Baumgart; Dr. Warren E. Burgess; Sorin Damian; George Dibley; Dr. Guido Dingerkus; Jeremy Dodd; John Dommers; Michael Gilroy; Burkhard Kahl; S. Kochetov; J. K. Langhammer; Dr. Sherman A. Minton; Aaron Norman; Peter W. Scott; Ruda Zukal.

© 1988 by T.F.H. Publications, Inc.

Distributed in the UNITED STATES by T.F.H. Publications, Inc., One T.F.H. Plaza, Neptune City, NJ 07753; in CANADA to the Pet Trade by H & L Pet Supplies Inc., 27 Kingston Crescent, Kitchener, Ontario N2B 2T6; Rolf C. Hagen Ltd., 3225 Sartelon Street, Montreal 382 Quebec; in CANADA to the Book Trade by Macmillan of Canada (A Division of Canada Publishing Corporation), 164 Commander Boulevard, Agincourt, Ontario M1S 3C7; in ENGLAND by T.F.H. Publications Limited, Cliveden House/Priors Way/Bray, Maidenhead, Berkshire SL6 2HP, England; in AUSTRALIA AND THE SOUTH PACIFIC by T.F.H. (Australia) Pty. Ltd., Box 149, Brookvale 2100 N.S.W., Australia; in NEW ZEALAND by Ross Haines & Son, Ltd., 18 Monmouth Street, Grey Lynn, Auckland 2, New Zealand; in SINGAPORE AND MALAYSIA by MPH Distributors (S) Pte., Ltd., 601 Sims Drive, #03/07/21, Singapore 1438; in the PHILIPPINES by Bio-Research, 5 Lippay Street, San Lorenzo Village, Makati Rizal; in SOUTH AFRICA by Multipet Pty. Ltd., 30 Turners Avenue, Durban 4001. Published by T.F.H. Publications, Inc. Manufactured in the United States of America by T.F.H. Publications, Inc.

Contents

Introduction

Nobody can really say what it is that attracts certain people to certain groups of animals. Most people have an affection for animals of one sort or another, and nearly everybody has kept something in captivity at some stage of their lives. As children, many people kept snails or beetles in glass jars; they later may have had a hamster, a guinea pig, or a rabbit—the more adventurous perhaps kept a turtle or a snake. Later on in life the majority of pet keepers settle for a dog, a cat, or perhaps a cage bird. All these little experiences with animals may develop into a specific interest in a particular group, and certain groups of dedicated keepers may be regarded as "specialists" by themselves or perhaps "eccentrics" by others. We are referring to those groups of people who have a love for the more unusual and exotic types of "pets." This book is for those who have a passion for the tailed amphibians, the salamanders and newts.

With ever-expanding urban areas and the influx of man into the cities to find work, people are gradually separating themselves from nature. This leads to a longing for some kind of substitute for nature, and many people opt to keep some kind of animal that can be kept in a miniature natural environment complete with plants and running water. Salamanders and newts are ideal choices for the home terrarium keeper—they are colorful, fairly easy to keep, and inexpensive to house. Moreover, there is still much to be learned about their various natural histories, an ideal opportunity for the amateur to become a scientist.

With a little artistic talent an attractive terrarium can be set up that will be the focal point of any living room or den. Providing the initial enthusiasm remains (and this should be carefully considered at the outset), and given a few basic requirements and a few minutes each day, it is easy to keep an exhibit of these animals that will be a sure topic of conversation whenever visitors arrive. The following text is designed to introduce the beginner to the fascinating world of salamanders and newts and gives guidelines on obtaining, housing, feeding, and caring for these fascinating creatures. It is hoped that this little book will lead the enthusiast into years of pleasure and entertainment.

EVOLUTION AND CLASSIFICATION

Whatever kind of animal you wish to keep in the home, you usually have the desire to delve into its background to find out as much as possible about the chosen pet. Not only does this give you a better "feel" for the little captives, it also gains you greater respect from your peers. This chapter contains information that is not strictly necessary to enable the beginner to successfully keep salamanders and newts in captivity, but such information will greatly enhance the interest of the newcomer to the hobby who desires to know more about these fascinating creatures.

Representatives of the other two living orders of Amphibia: a caecilian (Dermophis mexicanus) *above and a frog (Agalychnis annae) below.*

Evolution of the Amphibia
Salamanders and newts are in the order Amphibia along with the frogs and toads and the caecilians (logless tropical amphibians such as *Typhlonectes* and *Gymnopis*). These are the living representatives of the first group of vertebrates (animals with backbones) to colonize the dry land. Before amphibians moved onto land, the land had been the realm of only plants and invertebrates, notably some early insects. The first vertebrates were primitive fishes that were totally adapted to an aquatic existence. As numerous

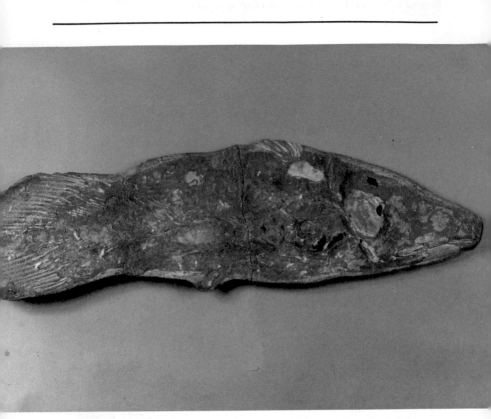

A fossil lobe-fin fish or crossopterygian, Axelrodichthys araripensis. *A fish perhaps similar to this is a remote ancestor of the amphibians.*

different species of fish evolved, competition grew rapidly. At the same time, some bodies of water began to dry up or were displaced by land movements. For these reasons certain groups of fishes, notably the ancestors of the living lungfishes and the crossopterygian or lobe-finned fishes (including the coelacanth), developed means of respiring atmospheric oxygen rather than extracting this life-supporting gas from the water by using only gills, as was the method used by other fish species. Over periods of millions of years primitive lungs developed, enabling these fishes to survive in waters not suitable for more conventional species. They were even able to survive for long periods in areas where the water had all but dried up.

Toward the latter part of

the Devonian period, some 350 million years ago, some of the crossopterygian fishes came out onto the land. It is very likely that these fishes were of a type represented by the genus *Eustenopteron*. In evolutionary terms, this was one of the boldest steps in history: a venturing of early vertebrates into a completely new environment to which they were only partially adapted. Once this step had been made, however, it was not long before these advanced, air-breathing fishes became transformed into primitive Amphibia.

From available fossil evidence it has been calculated that the earliest amphibians belonged to a group known as ichthyostegids, creatures that had characteristics of both the crossopterygian fishes and the later, more advanced amphibians. A typical ichthyostegid, a member of the genus *Ichthyostega*, had a skull about 15 cm (6 in) in length. Although similar in many respects to the skull of its crossoptergian fish ancestor, there were certain important changes between that of the fish and that of the amphibian. In the fish, for example, the part of the skull in front of the eyes was comparatively short, while the portion behind the eyes was comparatively long. In *Ichthyostega* a paradoxical situation prevailed in which the portion of the skull behind the eyes was relatively shorter than that of the fishes and the portion in front relatively longer. In amphibians, the eyes tended to be oriented more toward the top of the skull than in the fishes. Although *Ichthyostega* had developed strong pectoral and pelvic girdles that carried completely developed limbs and feet, the fin rays of the fish tail were retained! From this early fish/amphibian we can follow the evolution of the later amphibians as they radiated into different lines.

In changing from a totally aquatic existence to a new terrestrial life, various problems had to be resolved. While a fish normally obtains its oxygen from water by means of gills, the early amphibians had to further develop and perfect the lungs that they had inherited from their crossopterygian ancestors, although in the larval stage (as is still the case with modern amphibians) they continued to respire by means of gills. Another problem that land-dwelling animals had to deal with was the possibility of desiccation or drying up. To the fish this is no problem as it is continually bathed by the fluid in which it lives, but to land-dwelling creatures it is a major problem. The amphibians are faced with the necessity of retaining their body fluids while no longer immersed in the water. It can be inferred that the earliest amphibians, *Ichthyostega* for example, never ventured very far away from lakes and rivers to which they returned at frequent intervals, a habit that has followed through to most of today's amphibians. Certain branches of these early amphibians evolved more and more efficient ways of conserving water in the body, however, and these were the precursors of the reptiles, from which the birds and the mammals ultimately arose.

Another problem that arises from life on land is the influence of gravity. Whereas fishes are supported by the dense water in which they live and have developed a system of locomotion through body movements and fin stabilization, the first land-dwelling vertebrates had to evolve a system of moving over the land and supporting the body in the relatively thin atmosphere. A strong backbone and sturdy limbs were developed in the earliest stages of their evolution. The vertebral column was supported by a pectoral girdle at the front (which in turn was supported by the arms and the hands) and a pelvic girdle at the rear part of the body (which was supported by the legs and the feet). These limbs served not only to hold the body in counter-reaction to gravitational pull, but were the means by which the animal could propel itself over the land surface. The early amphibians retained a tail, which probably functioned as an organ of balance. In addition, the tail could still be used as an organ of propulsion when the animal returned to a watery environment. Although amphibians made a major contribution to life on land, they never really found a satisfactory solution to terrestrial reproduction. Throughout their history these animals have had to return to water or at least damp areas in order to lay their eggs.

From the original ichthyostegids a number of lines evolved that not only eventually led to our modern amphibians but also radiated into the ancestral lines of reptiles, birds, and mammals. Most of the earlier amphibians were large salamander-like creatures, including the leptospondyles—from which the lines leading to modern caecilians and caudates (tailed amphibians) developed—and the labyrinthodonts—from which the line leading to modern anurans (frogs and toads) developed. (Many herpetologists today believe that frogs, caudates and caecilians share a common ancestor rather than evolving from two separate groups of early amphibians.)

A large gap in geological time separates the leptospondyles and labyrinthodonts from the modern salamanders and frogs. The first frog-like creatures appeared in the early Triassic period, about 225 million years ago. While frogs have evolved to take up a great many habitats on land, the salamanders have retained a great many superficially primitive amphibian characteristics and have in the main

*These tiger salamander larvae (*Ambystoma tigrinum*) will develop the front legs before the hind ones erupt, a major and obvious difference from frog tadpoles.*

remained more dependent on a watery environment than have the anurans.

Classification
There are about 4000 known species of amphibians living on earth today, most of which are frogs and toads. The modern salamanders and newts (the caudates or Caudata) constitute just a small part of the class Amphibia, with about 350 species confined to the Americas and the temperate zones of Europe, Asia, and North Africa.

When one takes into consideration the total numbers of amphibian species and all of the other groups of animals and plants (totalling well over a million species), it is not surprising that a certain amount of confusion existed (and to some extent still does in many cases) among scientists who were

A typical salamander, a tiger salamander, Ambystoma tigrinum velasci. The subspecific name, velasci, indicates that this specimen comes from Mexico and has a distinctive color pattern typical of its subspecies.

endeavoring to sort out the species into some kind of logical categorization. Fortunately, a system was developed that has solved the vast majority of the problems, this being known as the *binomial* system of scientific nomenclature, in which each distinct species (the most natural and basic group, consisting of individuals which are very similar and which freely interbreed) is awarded a double scientific name. The system was pioneered by the Swedish biologist Carl von Linné (1707-1778), generally known as Linnaeus. Basically, the system dictated that each species described to science should be given a generic and a specific name. As an example, the tiger salamander is known scientifically as *Ambystoma tigrinum*, the first name being that of the genus, the second that of the species. There are other species of the genus *Ambystoma* (*Ambystoma maculatum, Ambystoma opacum, Ambystoma gracile*, and so on), and all of these species show certain similarities of structure that warrant their being placed in the same genus.

Genera (plural of genus) are grouped into larger categories in ascending sequence: the family, the order, the class, and so on. To illustrate the situation more clearly, the following table shows the classification of a single species, the tiger salamander, *Ambystoma tigrinum*:

Kingdom: Animalia, all animals. Phylum: Chordata, all chordates. Subphylum: Vertebrata, all vertebrates. Superclass: Tetrapoda, limbed vertebrates. Class: Amphibia, all amphibians. Order: Caudata, salamanders. Family: Ambystomidae, mole salamanders. Genus: *Ambystoma*, typical mole salamanders. Species: *Ambystoma tigrinum*, tiger salamander. Subspecies: *A. t. tigrinum*, eastern tiger salamander. Subspecies: *A. t. mavortium*, barred tiger salamander. Subspecies: *A. t. californiense*, California tiger salamander. Subspecies: *A. t. melanostictum*, blotched tiger salamander.

In the table, it will be seen that the basic species type is *Ambystoma tigrinum*. This species has been selected as an example due to the fact that it has many subspecies, a few of which are listed (there are no subspecies in many species). In cases where geographical races are different but not different enough to warrant separate specific rank in the opinion of

What's in a name? This pair of Triturus vulgaris *are readily recognized by the scientific name, but they are known by a variety of common names in different countries and languages. Americans call them European common newts.*

an expert, a subspecific name is added to the binomial, thus making it a trinomial. In such cases, the first described population of the species becomes representative of species and has its specific name simply repeated thus: *Ambystoma tigrinum tigrinum* (or, more conveniently, *A. t. tigrinum*), while further races described will receive a different subspecific name (e.g., *A. t. mavortium*, etc.). Subspecies will freely interbreed with each other where their natural ranges overlap. They usually interbreed when brought together in captive conditions, but this has little to do with their status as species or subspecies. Hybrids resulting from intersubspecific matings are called *intergrades* and may resemble either of the parents, may possess characteristics of both, or may (very rarely) have a totally different appearance. Natural intergrades sometimes pose taxonomic problems for field researchers. The question of subspecies is a touchy one with many herpetologists, and beginners are best advised to try to ignore them if at all possible.

In normal literature the generic, specific, and subspecific names are universally italicized (or underlined in the absence of italic script). Most scientific names are derived from classical Latin or Greek, as these were the main languages used by learned scholars at the time of the inception of the binomial system. To the modern salamander fancier it may seem rather superfluous to

The fire salamander, Salamandra salamandra, *belongs to the family Salamandridae, which contains mostly newts. A newt is just a name applied highly selectively to some aquatic salamanders.*

bother to learn the Latin names of various species when we have perfectly good English ones to use. By using Latin names, however, we can not only overcome the boundaries of language (scientific names being universal), we can also overcome the problems posed by a species being called a different name in the same language. For example *Triturus vulgaris* is called Teichmolch (pond newt) in Germany, common newt in England, and in the U.S.A. it is called the European common newt. It cannot be called plain common newt in the U.S.A. as it is certainly not common there, being represented by other species. It is therefore highly recommended that anyone who wants to make a hobby of keeping salamanders and newts make an effort to learn a little about their classification.

BIOLOGY OF SALAMANDERS AND NEWTS

The life history of the average frog is known by every school child, but for some unknown reason rather less seems to be known about the biology of the tailed amphibians. In this book we are not so concerned with the internal anatomy and physiology of the caudates as with their behavioral biology. In order to keep them alive in our terraria and encourage them to reproduce, it is most important that we know what makes them tick and what influences their breeding cycles.

Let us first endeavor to explain the differences between "salamanders" and "newts." There is no hard and fast distinction between the two types, and species commonly called newts and those commonly called salamanders may even belong to the same family. The term *salamander*, however, may be safely applied to all of the caudates, while *newt* is normally applied to certain semi-aquatic species which live on land from late summer through winter but enter water in the spring to breed; male newts often have elaborate breeding dress and courtship behavior. In Europe the newts are represented most commonly by salamanders of the genus *Triturus*, in North America by members of the genera *Notophthalmus* and *Taricha*, and in Asia by *Cynops, Paramesotriton, Tylototriton*, and others.

The salamanders and newts of the order Caudata comprise some 350 species belonging to eight families. They are found in North and South America (with a preponderance of species in the north), in Europe and North Africa, and in Asia, predominantly in the north temperate zones. They are absent from tropical parts of Asia and Africa and do not occur at all in Australasia.

The salamanders have a soft, moist skin, rather long bodies, and well developed tails. As the body regions are distinct and the front and hind legs are usually of similar size and well developed, salamanders are often mistaken for lizards. However, on closer examination it will be seen that they lack the scaly skin, claws, and external ear openings of the lizards. All salamanders (sirens are partially herbivorous) and their larvae are carnivorous. The smaller species feed upon insects and other available invertebrates, but the largest ones can take any small vertebrate they can overpower, including fish, frogs, and other

Salamander larvae are carnivorous, sometimes even cannibalistic. This axolotl larva eats mostly tubifex worms but will even take ground meat.

salamanders. All salamanders are secretive in their habits, and most are nocturnal. Unlike their close relatives the frogs, they are voiceless (with a few exceptions that may let out a sort of "squeak" of protest on being handled or attacked by a predator). They may be totally aquatic, semi-aquatic, or totally terrestrial, depending upon the species.

A wide range of breeding behavior is displayed by the various salamander species. Courtship displays may vary from simple affairs to quite elaborate ceremonies. With the exception of the giant

Asian salamanders (*Andrias*) and the North American hellbender (*Cryptobranchus*), fertilization is internal, but is accomplished without copulation. A gelatinous pyramidal structure, the spermatophore is deposited by the male in a suitable spot. The spermatophore is capped by a packet of spermatozoa that is retrieved by the receptive female with her cloacal lips. The spermatophore dissolves in the body but the sperm are stored for later use. As the eggs are laid, they are fertilized by individual sperm. In most cases the eggs are laid in water (many plethodontid species being exceptions to this), often attached individually to leaves of aquatic vegetation where they soon develop a protective jelly-like capsule. Some species "lay" free-swimming larvae that have developed within the female's body; others produce small versions of the adults that may be born directly on the land. Many woodland salamander species do not lay their eggs in water, but deposit them in some suitable sheltered and damp cavity. The young that hatch from these terrestrial eggs bypass the larval stage and hatch as miniature replicas of the adults.

The larvae of water-breeding species are entirely carnivorous and start feeding upon tiny aquatic animals within hours of hatching. At first the larvae are similar to the tadpoles of frogs but possess more conspicuous feathery external gills on either side of the head. They do not develop the large head of the anuran larva, however, and the front limbs develop before the hind ones (hind before front in frogs). As examples, let us take a more detailed look at the life histories of two species, the great crested newt, *Triturus cristatus*, and the fire salamander, *Salamandra salamandra*.

Life History of *Triturus cristatus*

Triturus cristatus is one of those species normally called a newt. Although it may be almost totally aquatic in some parts of its range, it is best known for entering breeding ponds in the spring after spending a period of hibernation in a deep cavity during the winter. The breeding season varies with the part of the range, but in central Europe the newts enter the breeding ponds in about mid-March to early

April. The breeding ponds must be fairly deep, clear water ponds with a good growth of aquatic vegetation. Breeding newts take on brighter colors, and the males in particular become living rainbows. The male develops a high, spiky crest that extends from just behind the head to the base of the tail, where there is a deep indentation. The crest continues, less spiky, along both the upper and lower edges of the broad, flat tail. A light blue or white band develops toward the center of the tail. The normally dark, almost black body becomes

A very young larva of the European crested newt, Triturus cristatus.

light brown with dark blotches and a scattering of tiny white spots along the flanks. The belly color, which is retained throughout the year, is yellow to bright orange-red, with black spots or blotches.

When the amorous male in his breeding dress finds a female who is prepared to witness his courtship dance, which normally takes place in an open weed-free "arena," he approaches her and nudges her body to attract her attention. If uninterested, she will simply swim away, but if receptive she will stay her ground and await further developments. The male may "rub noses" with the female before commencing to bend his body into a tight bow, the tip of the tail pointing in the direction of his prospective mate. He will place his two front feet firmly onto the substrate or onto a weed frond to give him stability, then proceed to rapidly wriggle the rear part of his body and tail. In so doing he releases an "aphrodisiac" scent from his cloaca and wafts it in the direction of the female with the water currents created by his actions. The male's dance may continue at intervals for many minutes, until the female seems to become hypnotized by his attentions.

He finally deposits a spermatophore in front of the female, who maneuvers her vent over it and absorbs the sperm-carrying material into her cloaca. She is now ready to fertilize the eggs, which will be reaching full development shortly.

After mating, the male shows no further interest in the female, who will then go off to lay her eggs. These are deposited singly on the leaves of water plants. Selecting individual leaves, the female will lay each egg on the underside and bend the foliage around to afford protection. The eggs develop a thin, sticky, jelly-like coating and adhere quite firmly to the leaves. In a few days the tiny larvae will have developed and will begin to hatch. At first they are completely legless, about 8 mm (3/8 in) in length, and possess three pairs of feathery gills just behind the head. As soon as the yolk sac is absorbed from the egg, the little newt tadpoles will begin to hunt for the minute aquatic organisms upon which they will voraciously feed. In most cases the larvae will develop into recognizable little newts by the end of the summer and will, like the adults, leave the water to seek their fortunes on the dry land.

Newts of all ages hunt for

This strikingly marked specimen is a recently metamorphosed juvenile of Triturus cristatus. *Fully matured adults are quite different.*

insects in the undergrowth for the remaining part of the summer and early autumn, usually confining their activities to the nighttime or dusk and dawn. During the day both adults and newly metamorphosed young will hide in some safe cavity, perhaps under or within rotten fallen timber, under rocks, or in the leaf litter. The adults lose their breeding dress during the terrestrial stage, the male losing his crest and dorsal pattern, becoming plain black above but retaining the bright orange and black belly.

Many species of newts and salamanders possess bright colors that act as a warning to predators that they are poisonous or distasteful.

Most species have glands in the skin that will release poisonous or irritant substances in times of danger. It is therefore advisable to wash your hands each time after handling salamanders, as these substances, if transferred to the eyes or mucous membranes, can cause severe pain, irritation, and inflammation.

As the winter approaches, in most parts of its range *T. cristatus* will prepare for its winter hibernation, a period that is important to prepare it for the forthcoming breeding season. The newts burrow deeply into the earth, often using tree roots or the burrows of other animals, until they reach a depth that will remain frost-free throughout the winter. Before hibernating, it is important that the newts have built up their fat reserves by consuming large quantities of insects. (Species from temperate areas may be kept in captivity without hibernation by simply keeping them warm, but such specimens are less likely to breed in the spring and their life spans will be somewhat shortened.) In the spring, as soon as the rays of the sun begin to warm up the surface, the newts will wake up and make their way to the breeding ponds. Young *T. cristatus* do not normally breed until they are in their second season.

Life History of *Salamandra salamandra*

The European fire salamander was probably the "original" salamander and can be described as a more typical salamander when compared to a newt (although both *Salamandra* and the newts belong to the same family, Salamandridae). This species, with its vivid orange-yellow and black coloration, was much feared

Developing fertile egg of Triturus vulgaris.

Newly hatched larvae of Triturus vulgaris.

leave their places of concealment and make a rapid attempt to escape, thus giving rise to the legend that the fire itself was the creator of these creatures.

Unlike the newts, the fire salamander does not enter the water to breed and the male does not develop any special kind of breeding dress, although the normal pattern of black and orange or bright yellow blotches or stripes is vivid enough. Living in damp, usually forested areas rarely far from water, the salamanders emerge in spring from their hibernating places in deep leaf litter or

One-month-old larva of Triturus vulgaris with hind legs.

and features largely in ancient European folklore. It was said to be "born of the fire" and was credited with mystical powers that varied from region to region. The fire-birth theory probably rose from the fact that these salamanders commonly hide during the day under or within rotten logs that might be collected for fireplaces. As soon as the heat of the fire became unbearable, the salamanders would of course hollows among the roots of trees. Pairing may take place throughout the warmer months and usually occurs in damp situations on land, although it has been observed in shallow water. The male forces himself under the female from the rear until he is almost carrying her on his back. He holds her tightly by entwining his legs with hers and rubs his head against her throat and strokes her cloaca with his tail. The male gradually becomes more and more excited during his movements and eventually deposits a spermatophore on the substrate. He then releases the rear portion of the female's body and moves to the left or to the right so that

Fully matured late larvae of Triturus vulgaris. *The gills have virtually disappeared and the legs are fully developed.*

Salamandra salamandra *is one of the few salamanders that gives live birth. Actually, this varies quite a bit from population to population.*

his mate can have access to the sperm packet. Lying quietly, the male allows her to maneuver her vent over the sperm packet and take it up in the lips of her cloaca. The mating process takes approximately half an hour, after which the female is released by the male and both go their separate ways.

The time from fertilization to the birth of the larvae is about ten months. Sometimes the sperm packet may be retained in the cloaca for several months, even through the winter, so that eggs may be fertilized at a more favorable time. The larvae develop full term in the eggs while still in the body of the parent, who will seek out a suitable body of water as

soon as birth becomes imminent. Only cool streams and ponds in half shadow are selected. The female will search for a suitable shallow spot into which she can release up to 50 hatching eggs or newly hatched larvae. In certain cases, especially in the southern part of the range or where free water is scarce, the larvae may be retained right through metamorphosis and tiny replicas of the adults may be deposited.

At birth, the larvae are about 2.5 cm (1 in) in length and are colored somewhere between yellowish gray and brownish black. The body is usually speckled with little yellow spots, with a larger one at the base of each leg;

the latter spot is a trademark of *S. salamandra* larvae and is not present in the larvae of related species. The larvae possess a pair of feathery gills just like those of *Triturus* species, but the salamander larva is more robust in build. On reaching a length of 5–6 cm (2–2½ in) the larvae begin to develop the vivid coloration of the adults, at first slowly but more rapidly as time goes by. The gills begin to be absorbed, the flat swimming tail becomes rounded, and the amphibian metamorphoses to become ready for its terrestrial existence. It is impossible to give an exact period of time from birth to metamorphosis, although spring-born larvae will usually become terrestrial by autumn; those born later in the year may pass the winter as larvae and metamorphose in the spring of the following year.

On land the young salamanders will hunt, usually at dusk and in the darkness, for various small invertebrates that they will catch with their sticky, protrusible tongues. They may also be seen foraging on the forest floor after heavy rain during warm weather. Fire salamanders are rarely preyed upon by other creatures, their warning coloration indicating that they are distasteful, indeed poisonous, because of the toxic secretions of the skin glands.

This view of a late larval newt, Triturus vulgaris, *shows the gills, legs, and lateral line organs very well.*

HOUSING FOR SALAMANDERS

The keeping of any animal in captivity requires a responsible attitude. Unless you are certain that you will have the time, the devotion, and the ongoing enthusiasm for the hobby, then you should not start in the first place. Having decided to keep salamanders or newts in the home, the first step is to ensure that the correct type of housing is available. This should be done before any animals are acquired. The type of housing required will differ from species to species, depending on whether they are totally aquatic, semiaquatic, or terrestrial. A container in which living animals are kept is usually called an aquarium for aquatic creatures or a vivarium or terrarium for terrestrial creatures. For convenience, a container for semiaquatic animals is usually called an aqua-terrarium. Being amphibians, one may imagine that all newts and salamanders should be kept in an aquarium or aqua-terrarium, but this is not necessarily the case. Before deciding on a species to keep, make sure that you have a knowledge of its habits and native habitat so that conditions as natural as possible can be provided. Where it is impossible or extremely difficult to produce conditions that are totally natural, some acceptable compromise conditions can usually be found.

The Aquarium

We are here referring to the aquarium as a container of water in which we want to reproduce a totally aquatic environment with no land areas. Aquarium tanks may also be used for other types of housing. There are many kinds of tanks available on the market today, including molded clear plastic or plexiglass tanks that are usually small and ideal for rearing larvae and young newts. One disadvantage of plastic tanks, however, particularly if you want to use them as main display tanks, is that after continued use and cleaning a fine film of scratches will develop and eventually spoil the view into the vessel.

Another type of aquarium is the traditional iron- or steel-framed type into which panes of glass are fixed with putty. The disadvantage of these tanks is that, unless the frames are rust-proofed and painted at regular intervals with non-toxic paint, they will rust away. In addition, traditional putty tends to shrink and crack if the tank is stored without water, causing the tank to leak the next time it is filled.

By far the best type of tank available for general purposes is the all-glass tank. This consists of a number of sheets of glass of appropriate sizes cemented together along their edges with a remarkably versatile substance called silicone rubber sealing compound

An all-glass aquarium is the best and most simple container for virtually any salamander or newt.

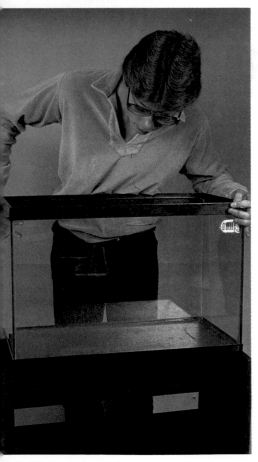

(silicone cement). This type of putty has various commercial uses, but brands suitable for aquarium construction are usually available at pet shops. All-glass aquaria are available in a wide array of sizes and designs at any pet shop, and it is usually cheaper to buy an all-glass tank than to try to make one yourself.

Great care should be taken in properly placing an aquarium for aquatic salamanders, remembering that a tank of water is extremely weighty. A sturdy base should be chosen and put in a quiet location away from a window and near an electrical outlet. Once in its permanent position, the tank should be thoroughly cleaned (without soaps) then filled with water and tested for leaks, which can be repaired with silicone cement.

Most of the smaller aquatic salamanders will appreciate a natural looking environment with plants, rocks, and other decorative materials. Good tips on setting up a planted aquarium can be obtained from books about keeping tropical or cold-water fishes. Here it will suffice to say that a layer of washed aquarium gravel about 5 cm (2 in) deep at the front of the tank, rising to about 7.5 cm (3 in) at the rear, should be placed in the aquarium. Non-toxic rocks

Some of the equipment, decorations, and live food you will need for keeping your newt or salamander in an aquarium or aqua-terrarium.

(granite, slate, etc., but not limestone) may be placed to form valleys, caves, and terraces. Various aquatic plants may be planted in the substrate (check with your pet shop for the best plants to use and how to grow them), usually with the smaller ones at the front and graduating to taller specimens at the rear and ends. Larger salamanders can be quite violent with their surroundings and will continually uproot weak plants, so only robust specimens should be used, these being allowed to establish strong root systems before any animals are introduced. Such aquaria are suitable for rearing the larvae of many species of salamanders and newts as well as for permanently keeping those forms that are totally aquatic.

The Aqua-terrarium

The aqua-terrarium is one that contains roughly equal land and water areas. Such containers are suitable for those salamanders that spend equal amounts of time on the land and in the water or those that spend the breeding season in an aquatic environment. An ordinary aquarium tank can be used. A partition of glass some 15 cm (6 in) high can be placed across the bottom of the tank and sealed into place to form a watertight barrier between the land and swimming areas. The substrate of the water area can be about 2.5 cm (1 in)

deep, thus leaving a water depth of about 12.5 cm (5 in). A rock gradient can be placed up the side of the glass partition to allow easy access and egress of the inmates. The land area is filled to about half with pebbles and coarse gravel to provide drainage. If possible, drainage holes should be made in the base of the land area to prevent excessive waterlogging. A mixture of garden loam, peat, and clean sand can be placed over the pebbles to bring the land up to water level. These materials should be sterilized to reduce the possibility of souring and molding. A slab of grassy turf can be placed over the whole land area (this can be changed at regular intervals) or green moss clumps can be used. For extra decoration a couple of dwarf potted plants can be sunk into the substrate, and mossy bark, stone caves, or pieces of broken clay flowerpots can be used to provide shelters for the inmates.

For those with greater ambition, a more natural aqua-terrarium can be made by using a very large tank and building up a rockery at the rear. The tank can be situated in an alcove in the house or conservatory. In such cases, the whole of the aquarium tank becomes the pond and the back wall is built up with natural rocks and cement to form a false river bank. Special cavities should be left between some of the rocks and filled with potting compost. Various semiaquatic plants may be installed in the "bank" area.

woodland species, which should breed readily in the water provided. One word of caution: when using cement in such a structure, fill the tank with water after the cement has set, then leave for 24 hours; then drain and scrub the cement surfaces. This should be done three or

The properly landscaped aqua-terrarium is not only attractive but it must also provide proper habitat and be easy to maintain.

The front of the display above the tank can be filled in with a sheet of glass mounted in a frame that can be opened for access. Above this, a further frame covered with fine mesh will provide ventilation. With careful artistic planning it is possible to create a really natural looking and attractive micro-habitat for your animals. Such a display will be ideal for many amphibious

four times until the lime deposits (which appear on the surface of the cement as a whitish film) are eliminated.

The Terrarium
The plain terrarium is used for those species that live in damp conditions but do not require larger bodies of water in which to breed. The substrate can be set up as described for the land area of

Heaters are necessary for some types of newts and aquatic salamanders. Submersible heaters are perhaps best because they are less obtrusive.

the aqua-terrarium, but free water is not strictly necessary for the welfare of the inmates. However, high humidity is essential and regular misting (with a plant sprayer) must be carried out. For safety's sake, it is advisable to have a small dish of water available at all times.

Life Support Systems

As well as the basic tank and its decorations, there are a number of life support systems that may be essential to the well-being of the inmates. These include heating, lighting, humidity, ventilation, and water filtration. All of these systems warrant discussion in some detail.

The Terrarium Lid: This not only prevents the inmates from escaping (some salamanders are extremely adept at crawling up a sheer glass surface because the slimy body secretions can produce suction), it forms a housing for the lighting system (and heating system if it is required) and provides ventilation. A terrarium lid may be made from plastic (common in purchased terraria) but also could be fashioned from plywood given a couple of coats of non-toxic gloss paint to render it damp-proof. A couple of large holes are made in the top of the lid and covered with a fine gauge mesh. The lid should be at least 15 cm (6 in) deep to allow for the lighting apparatus.

Heating: Very few salamanders other than those from tropical and subtropical areas will require supplementary heating other than that provided by the normal room temperatures of the average household. As tropical species also require a high humidity, it is best to install apparatus that will provide both warmth and moist air. One of the most satisfactory ways of heating small terraria is to use aquarium heaters of the type supplied for tropical fish tanks. There are many kinds available on the market, so visit your local pet shop to see what is being offered. Most aquarium heaters consist of a heating element in a heat-resistant glass tube with a waterproof stopper through which the power cable passes. A thermostat may be present as an integral part of the heater or it may come in a separate tube. The thermostat is, however, an essential part of the equipment.

In the aqua-terrarium the heater is simply placed in the water. This will often be sufficient (particularly in association with the lighting) to provide a satisfactory range of temperatures for both the water and the air (even tropical species will be content at temperatures not greater than 77°F). As the water is heated slow evaporation takes place, which will maintain a high humidity in the air space. In the dry land terrarium, which contains no large areas of water, the heater may be placed in the water dish or in a concealed jar of water placed in the rear of the tank.

Other forms of heating which may be used are heat cables (of the type used by horticulturists to warm soil), which may be placed in the substrate; heating pads, which may be placed under the terrarium; and heat lamps, which are best placed outside the terrarium and allowed to shine through the gauze of the lid (great care should be taken in the use of such lamps to avoid desiccation of the plants and animals)—the temperature can be adjusted by raising or lowering the lamp.

As amphibia are *ectothermic* (body temperature controlled by surrounding environmental temperature), they are able to maintain their preferred body temperature only by moving into or out of warm places. It is therefore advisable to have a range of temperatures available in the terrarium. This can be accomplished by placing the heating apparatus to one end or side; the warmest part will then be near the heater and the temperature will decrease gradually at greater distances away from it. The salamanders will then be able to seek out a spot in the terrarium where the temperature is most comfortable to them. Where aquarium heaters are used as the sole form of heating this temperature gradient is not so important; although the water will maintain a reasonably constant temperature, the air temperatre will vary with changes in the degree of ventilation.

In most countries there is a dropping of the temperature at night. It is advisable to reduce the temperature in the

If terraria containing tropical species are kept in unheated rooms where there is a danger of excessively low temperatures in the winter, then some form of supplementary heating must be provided. Another factor that must be taken into consideration is seasonal

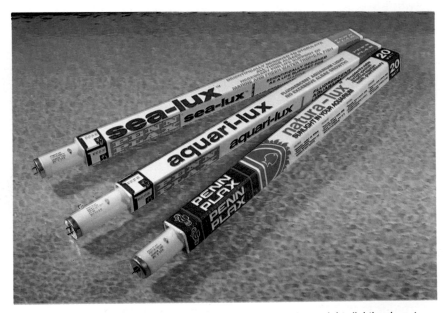

Since many salamanders are burrowers and active only at night, lighting is not always too important. However, newts need lighting that will allow the plants in their tank to grow well.

terrarium by as much as 10°C each night. This can be accomplished by simply switching off the heaters at night; the prevailing temperature in the average home will be adequate for the remainder of the night.

temperature variation. This is particularly important with temperate species, whose breeding cycles are controlled by environmental changes in the spring.

Lighting: Most salamanders, with the

possible exception of aquatic species during the breeding season, are nocturnal and prefer to keep out of the light during the day by hiding in nooks and crannies, under rocks, or in hollow logs. Photoperiod (daily duration of light) is important to many species in their normal lives and in their breeding cycles. Many temperate species come into breeding condition when influenced by increasing hours of daylight and increasing temperatures in the spring. It is advisable to try and reproduce a light/dark cycle similar to that found in the native habitat of the species in question. If more than one species is kept in a single terrarium, try to choose species that come from similar habitats and climatic areas. It is advisable to use artificial lighting in indoor terraria as sunlight entering through the glass can soon raise the temperature to lethal levels unless great care is taken.

If plants are to flourish in the terrarium, a good quality artificial light is required. Suitable lights are available from lighting specialists, pet shops, and horticultural suppliers in the form of broad-spectrum fluorescent tubes that emit a quality of light ideal for plant growth. These tubes come under

Automatic water changers have made life much easier for the hobbyist who keeps newts and other aquatic salamanders. Although as a rule newts are not excessively sensitive to pollution, their plants are.

certain trade names and are available in various wattages and sizes suitable for all kinds of terraria. The lamps can be mounted in special brackets in the aquarium lid, but they must be protected by gauze to prevent the inmates from coming into contact with them.

37

Ventilation: Although essential in the terrarium, good ventilation must be produced without creating excessive drafts. Good ventilation will prevent a buildup of foul, organism-laden air, remove excess carbon dioxide, and discourage the growth of unpleasant molds on the substrate. All lids to terraria must be adequately ventilated; the greater the vented area the better. In fact, a simple frame covered with fine plastic or metal mesh is ideal. For even more efficient ventilation, one or more of the sides or parts of the sides of the terrarium can have the glass replaced by acrylic or plexiglass panels into which rows of small holes about 6 mm (1/4 in) in diameter are neatly drilled.

Another method of improving the ventilation in the terrarium is to install an aquarium aeration pump. These pumps are available in various sizes, but a small diaphragm pump will be adequate for a medium sized terrarium. A plastic tube is run from the pump, which is usually concealed somewhere outside the tank, into the water part of the terrarium. On the end of the tube is an airstone. When the pump is switched on, tiny bubbles of air will rise to the water surface, creating air movement in the terrarium. In fact, such a system will perform a number of additional functions. An air pump is essential if gilled larvae are being kept or reared as it will aerate the water (by a combination of bubbles and water current) and increase the oxygen supply. It will also help keep the water "sweet," create ventilation, increase humidity, and, if the water is heated, it will help raise the temperature of the air. Such aerators are useful in operating filters and creating waterfalls.

Humidity: Humidity in the air is essential to most amphibians. We should aim to have a level of 60% or more in the average terrarium for terrestrial salamanders. The use of an air pump will help keep levels up, but it may be necessary to mist the terrarium interior one or more times per day, depending on how dry is the outside atmosphere. Salamanders and newts will quickly desiccate and die where humidity is inadequate. A mist sprayer of the type used by horticulturists is ideal for use in the terrarium.

Filtration: It is highly recommended that a water filter is used in the aquarium and aqua-terrarium. Many species will quickly foul the water, which will not only become evil-smelling, it will soon become unhygienic and even toxic to the inmates. The simplest type of filter is that known as the *airlift*. This is operated by the air pump and consists of a plastic box that is filled with a filter medium such as nylon floss. It works on the principle that rising air bubbles create a current. The airstone is passed to the bottom of the tube in the center of the filter box. As the air rises, it creates a current that continually pulls water through the filter medium, removing the suspended solids. Such a filter is adequate for a small volume of water, but the filter modium must be changed frequently.

For larger volumes of water a power filter is recommended. There are several types available, but the majority consist of robust pumps that remove the water from the tank and force it through a filter medium (which may consist of various layers of filter media and chemicals for purifying the water). Power filters should be used according to the manufacturer's instructions. By clever use of filters, the returning water can be made to run back into the tank via a rock wall, thus creating a

Power filters are very useful if you are trying to keep large, mossy salamanders or high concentrations of smaller species. In an aquarium the wastes can accumulate rapidly.

miniature waterfall that will also increase humidity levels in the air. For more details of various filters, it is recommended that the reader refer to a good book on the maintenance of a tropical fish aquarium.

Greenhouse Accommodations

Many species of newts and salamanders, particularly

those from subtropical areas, are suitable for keeping in conservatories and greenhouses. In such cases they are given the free run of the area and, providing the correct type of breeding pool is available, they should reproduce almost naturally. Even tropical species can be kept in this way, if you can afford to heat your greenhouse to "tropical" temperatures (fortunately there are almost no tropical-temperature salamanders, as even the Central and South American species inhabit cool microhabitats). All windows and doors must be covered with insect screening to prevent the inmates from escaping.

A garden pool housing salamanders can be colorful as well as interesting.

Outdoor Accommodations

Native salamanders can be encouraged to live in your garden by simply providing them with a suitable breeding pond (if necessary) and adequate hiding areas. Initial stocking is done by adding wild-collected eggs or larvae to the pond or introducing adult woodland salamanders to moist debris piles. Providing conditions are suitable and there is adequate vegetative cover, the newts will metamorphose and stay in the area, probably breeding in the same pond when they reach maturity. It is usually a waste of time trying to do this if you also keep fish in the pond as the latter will eat the larvae; you can only concentrate on one or the other.

For more confined outdoor housing a fence may be built around the pond and the land area. Be sure that there is an overhang at the top of the fence to prevent the inmates from climbing out. Such an enclosure is one of the best methods of keeping and breeding native species in controlled conditions. The enclosure may be attractively landscaped with rocks, plants, old logs, and perhaps a waterfall with various ponds at different levels, giving your newts or salamanders a choice of breeding sites.

FOODS AND FEEDING

All animals, whether they are human beings, elephants, mice, ants, or salamanders, require what is termed a *balanced diet* for their basic metabolism to function correctly. To obtain a balanced diet, an animal has to consume foods that contain the correct proportions of at least the basic nutritive ingredients, these being proteins, carbohydrates, fats, vitamins, and minerals. All salamanders and newts are carnivorous in that they eat other animals (usually invertebrates in the majority of cases). They are fairly catholic in their diet, consuming a wide range of insects, spiders, worms, and so on. Some of the larger species will take small vertebrates, including other amphibians and reptiles. Vegetable material is not deliberately consumed by most species (except

One of the best ways to get live food for salamanders is to turn over logs. There you will find not only little things to be used as food, but odd and often colorful animals such as this beautiful millipede.

possibly in the early larval stage of some species and the sirens), but a certain amount may be taken in during the capture of prey or in the undigested contents of the prey animal's gut. In the wild, salamanders and newts obtain a balanced diet by consuming a variety of organisms. Temperate species that hibernate in the winter months must also take in sufficient reserves of nutrients to take them through the period of hibernation and prepare them for the spring breeding season.

In the wild, most species will take livefoods only. Terrestrial species usually react to the sight of movement to detect the prey. In aquatic salamanders movement, odor, or touch may attract the predator to its prey, which explains why carrion may be eaten in the wild or strips of meat or fish in captivity. In captivity it is a great temptation to give salamanders the most easily available foods, such as mealworms, that may be purchased conveniently and regularly. Although mealworms are an excellent food taken readily by many medium to large salamanders, there is evidence that they are lacking in certain minerals that are important to metabolism and should therefore be given only as *part* of a more varied diet.

Collecting Livefoods

Although there are several species of invertebrates that can be purchased at regular intervals or cultured in the home, the collection of a varied supply from the wild is highly recommended. Not only will this provide your captives with a greater variety in their diet, it will help to relieve "boredom" to a certain extent (even salamanders and newts can get "fed up" with the same old items on the menu). One of the most productive methods of obtaining a selection of terrestrial insects and spiders is by "sweeping" herbage with a large canvas-reinforced insect net (called, logically, a sweep net). The net is passed through the foliage of trees, shrubs, and tall grass, and the resulting catch is placed in jars or plastic containers to be transported home. Such sweepings during the summer months should provide a veritable potpourri of caterpillars, beetles, bugs, grasshoppers, and spiders. After grading to suitable sizes, these invertebrates will be eagerly taken by many species of terrestrial salamanders. Never place too many insects in the terrarium at any one time; allow the inmates to devour what is available before adding more, otherwise you may get an overpopulation of insect escapees in the house. In addition, excessive livefood items will eventually fall into the water, drown, and spoil.

Other good places for collecting invertebrate prey items include under rotten logs and other debris. Pillbugs, beetles, and earthworms can be collected in this way. For collecting larger numbers of insects from flowers, a "pooter" can be used. This is a glass or plastic bottle with a cork through which two tubes are passed, one of which has a flexible rubber tube attached to it. By placing the end of the rubber tube close to an insect and sucking sharply on to the other tube with the mouth, the insect will pass through the long tube and fall into the bottle. It is advisable to place a piece of cotton wool or fine screening over the mouthpiece to prevent insects being sucked accidentally into the mouth.

A good source of food for very small (newly metamorphosed) salamanders is aphids, which may often be found on new green shoots of domesticated plants. Sometimes these insects congregate in large numbers and it is a simple matter to pluck the whole shoot and place it in the terrarium. Small moths and other night-flying insects can be captured using a simple light-trap: a white sheet is suspended in a suitable place with a strong light shining onto it. The insects will be attracted to the sheet and can be usually easily caught and placed in a container.

For aquatic salamanders, including newts in their aquatic stage and larvae, various small aquatic invertebrates can be netted from ponds and streams. Daphnia or water fleas are small crustaceans that are abundant in waters with a good algal content during the summer months. These are ideal for feeding to larvae and smaller aquatic adults. They can often be purchased alive or frozen at your pet shop. Mosquito larvae, bloodworms, and glassworms are all free-swimming insect larvae that can be fed to aquatic species. When collecting aquatic livefoods one should be careful not to introduce carnivorous larvae such as those of dragonflies or water beetles, which could easily make a meal of tiny newt larvae. Brine shrimp nauplii and adults make an excellent food for aquatic salamanders; they can be cultured or purchased at your local pet shop.

Culturing Livefoods

Although it would be ideal if we could provide our salamanders with freshly livefoods can usually obtain regular supplies from a pet shop or by mail order, but it is often more economical and interesting to culture your own foods once you have the initial stock.

Mealworms: These are the larvae of the flour beetle *Tenebrio molitor*. For

Brine shrimp are perhaps the most readily available live food suitable for sala-manders and newts and are also the most readily cultured. They are also avail-able frozen and freeze-dried.

caught livefood all the year around, this is not always possible. We may not have enough time to spend each day collecting food, and colder areas have a distinct shortage of such foods in the winter. For staple diets we have to rely on cultured livefoods. Those who lack the time to culture their own generations they have been the most convenient and easily obtainable livefood for keepers of small carnivores. They can be purchased in small or large quantities from dealers, and it is a simple matter to breed and maintain a steady supply. Allow a number of mealworms to pupate and metamorphose

Adult mealworm beetles are foundation stock for a supply of mealworms that can be used for feeding larger and more sturdy types of salamanders. Mealworms are not recommended for smaller and delicate salamanders.

into adult beetles. These are brown and about 8 mm (³/₈ in) in length. The adult beetles are placed in containers with tight-fitting, ventilated lids along with a 5 cm (2 in) layer of food. A mixture of bran and crushed oats is ideal. A piece of burlap is placed over this and a couple of pieces of carrot or a similar vegetable are placed on top. The beetles will eat at the vegetables when they require moisture. The beetles will soon mate and lay eggs in the bran. These eggs will hatch and develop into full sized mealworms in about 16 weeks. By starting a new culture with about 100 beetles each month, a regular supply of mealworms of all sizes will be continually available. The extra adult beetles may also be fed to larger salamanders. The cultures are best kept in a temperature range of 25–30°C (77–86°F) for maximum results.

Crickets: In recent years cricket cultures have become increasingly popular as a source of food for captive insect-eating animals. There are several species available that may be cultured quite easily. An old aquarium tank with a tight-fitting, ventilated lid is ideal for cricket culture. A layer of clean sawdust is placed in the base and pieces of crumpled newspaper or torn-up egg boxes are placed

Crickets are readily digested, available in many sizes, and readily purchased or cultured. They are eaten by many types of salamanders and newts and can serve as the basic food for some.

about 15 mm (⅝ in). Crickets thus are a versatile livefood, being both nutritious and available in various sizes.

The complete life cycle of the cricket takes about three months. The young may be reared through their instars in the same way that the adults are kept. With careful planning, a breeding colony of crickets will provide a constant supply of nutritious livefood throughout the year. To catch them up from their container, take up the crumpled paper in which they are hiding and shake the required quantity into a jar (held over the container!). By placing the jar in a

at one end for the crickets to hide in. The crickets may be fed on a mixture of bran and crushed oats as well as the odd pieces of vegetable. A dish containing water-soaked cotton wool will provide the insects with drinking water. The adults are most likely to lay their eggs in this, so the pad of cotton wool and the dish should be moved to a separate container at regular intervals and replaced with a new one. The eggs will hatch in 21 days or less if they are maintained at a temperature of 25°C (77°F). The hatchling nymphs are suitable for very small salamanders as they are only about 3 mm (⅛ in) in length. There are four instars (nymphal stages), each one a little larger than the former, until the cricket reaches the adult size of

Cockroaches are cultured in some laboratories and are an excellent food for some salamanders. The decision to culture cockroaches at home should not be made lightly, however.

refrigerator for ten minutes or so, the crickets will be slowed down enough to prevent escapes when you are feeding them to your animals.

Grasshoppers: These are also available from specialist suppliers or may be caught locally. Although the adults are too large to feed to all but the biggest of salamanders,

bottle of water and pack wadding around the neck to prevent the insects from falling in and drowning. They are best kept in tall aquaria or glass-fronted boxes (ventilated). They lay their eggs in slightly moistened sand at a depth of about 2.5 cm (1 in), so they must be provided with containers in

Bloodworms are an excellent food greatly appreciated by many newts and other aquatic salamanders. They are readily purchased but cannot be cultured at home.

the various instar stages are useful for smaller species. Grasshoppers are a little more difficult to breed than crickets. They may be fed on a mixture of bran and crushed oats, supplemented by fresh greenfood that is changed daily. A convenient way of providing this food is to place grass stems in a

which to do this. They are best maintained at a temperature of about 28°C (82°F).

Flies: Various species of flies are an excellent food for salamanders, and there are sizes to suit all. The staple diet of some of the smallest newly metamorphosed salamanders has often been fruitflies (*Drosophila*), those little pests that colonize rotting fruit. A colony can soon be started in the summer by placing a box of banana skins or rotten fruit in some corner of the garden (preferably well away from the house!). This will be teeming with flies in no time at all. The flies may be collected from the area by using a fine-meshed net.

Fruitflies are used extensively in laboratories for genetic experiments. There they are cultured in jars of a medium based on agar jelly. Many different strains of fruitflies are available from biological supply houses (see your college biology department) and livefood dealers. For small terrestrial salamanders, the wingless (vestigial) variety of fruitfly is very useful.

The lesser housefly, *Fannia canicularis*, and the common housefly, *Musca domestica*, are useful for small to medium salamanders, while the greenbottles, *Lucilia*, and bluebottles, *Calliphora*, are suitable for larger ones. Many flies can be caught during the summer in a flytrap. This consists basically of a cubical framework (about 30 × 30 × 30 cm—12 × 12 × 12 in) covered with fine mesh gauze. This is mounted on a flat board with a 5 cm (2 in) hole in the center, over which is placed a transparent funnel with a spout of sufficient width to let the flies through. The whole trap is placed on four stones so that the board is raised about 5 cm (2 in) above the ground. A piece of strong-smelling meat or fish is placed under the hole in the board. The flies will be attracted to the bait by smell and will crawl under the board to feed and lay eggs. When disturbed, they will make for the nearest source of light, which is through the hole and funnel, where they will be trapped behind the gauze screen. The flies can be extracted by having a muslin sleeve on one side of the frame so that a jar can be passed into the trap. When not in use the sleeve is knotted at the end.

A more convenient method of obtaining a supply of flies is to purchase maggots, which are sometimes available in bait shops. The maggots can be placed in small containers of bran or sawdust, where they will pupate in a few days. In another few days the adult flies will emerge. By having a fly-sized hole in the lid of the container, the flies will escape singly. The whole container may be placed in the terrarium, where the

Waxmoth larvae are not that well known in the United States but are a standard food in Europe. Cultures may be available at pet shops and the larvae are sometimes sold in bait shops. The cultures are not very easy to maintain.

inmates will soon learn the source of food and wait around the hole for the flies to emorge. Maggots sold as bait are often called "gentles."

Earthworms: These are a highly nutritious food eagerly taken by many salamanders. Earthworms come in various sizes depending on their stages of growth. A good method of ensuring a fairly continuous supply of earthworms in the summer months is to clear a patch of earth in some corner of the garden, preferably where it is shaded from the sun. Place a 5 cm (2 in) layer of dead leaves over this and peg out a large piece of burlap sacking over the leaves. The sacking

is then well dampened with water (but not waterlogged) every day. By looking under the sacking and sorting through the leaves at regular intervals, a good supply of earthworms of all sizes should be forthcoming for several weeks. As the supply diminishes, the collecting area can be moved elsewhere.

Whiteworms: These are slender whitish worms that grow to about 2 cm (¾ in) in length. Normally found among decaying vegetation, they can be purchased from many pet shops as cultures. They are placed in preferably sterilized loam in a flat box such as a seed tray, and a few small pieces of stale bread or a few spoonsful of crushed oats are placed in depressions in the surface of the soil. The whole surface is then dampened by misting at daily intervals and covered with a sheet of glass. The culture should be kept in a dark spot at a temperature of around 22°C (72°F). The worms will breed rapidly and congregate around the food patches, where they may be teased out with a camel's hair brush at regular intervals. As such cultures tend to sour or mold quickly, it is recommended that a new culture is started at two-week intervals until one has four cultures going, each one being discarded at eight weeks of age and being replaced by a new one. Worms from the oldest culture can be used to start the next one.

Supplements

Salamanders that receive a great variety of food items are unlikely to suffer from vitamin or mineral deficiencies. However, occasions arise, particularly during the winter months, when non-hibernating species have to be given cultured livefoods such as mealworms or crickets over long periods. In such cases it is highly recommended that a multivitamin/mineral supplement be given at regular intervals (say at two or three times per week). Multivitamin liquids and powders are available from your local pet shop. For amphibians, powdered forms

Undoubtedly one of the finest and most acceptable foods for virtually all salamanders is the common earthworm. Actually, the common earthworm can be any of several dozen species depending on where they are collected, but almost all are excellent food. Small specimens and species are best, as larger worms will have to be chopped up. Earthworms are readily purchased and also readily cultured even indoors.

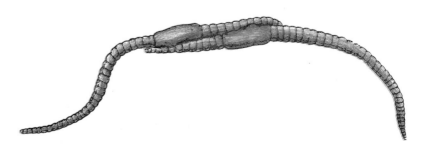

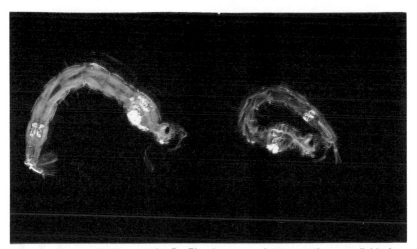

Glassworms are the larvae of a fly, Chaoborus, *and are sometimes available for sale in pet shops. They could never provide a steady diet for newts or their larvae.*

are most suitable as they can be dusted directly onto the livefood.

Feeding Strategies

Most species of salamanders can be fed on a daily basis, giving them just as much food as they can manage at one time. The correct amounts of food to give will have to be ascertained by experimentation, but it is better to give too little rather than too much, particularly with aquatic species, where uneaten food will soon foul the water. With terrestrial species, it will do no harm if a few living insects are in the cage for a few days, but no further food items should be given until the original ones have been eaten (after ensuring, of course, that what you have given is accepted as a food item).

Most species of terrestrial salamander are initially attracted to their prey by its movement, so in the majority of cases it is a waste of time giving dead food. However, some of the larger species can be persuaded to take tiny pieces of lean raw meat by placing it in front of them and jiggling it about with a very fine straw (a straw from a broom is ideal). Aquatic species will find food by a combination of touch and odor, so they can be given an occasional piece of meat, fish, or shellfish. Such foods, however, do not constitute a balanced diet and should only be used as "fillers" when livefood is not available.

Selection of Specimens

One of the most important aspects of keeping animals is to ensure that one starts off with healthy stock. When purchasing from a dealer, first impressions of the premises can give one a good idea as to the likely state of health of the animals in stock. Dirty, smelly, untidy premises with overstocked terraria are more likely to harbor disease organisms than establishments whose proprietors obviously go out of their way to provide their stock with all the necessary requirements and display it in a manner designed to impress the customer.

Select specimens that are plump (sunken abdomens and exaggeration of the bones in the pelvic area are sure signs of malnutrition) and have an unblemished skin. The eyes should be open and bright. Avoid specimens with dull or cloudy

If you collect your own specimens, first make sure that you can legally keep them. Many laws now apply to collecting almost all reptiles and amphibians. Choose only perfect specimens of species that will make satisfactory pets. Few burrowing species can be kept for long.

eyes and those which show any sign of inflammation. Specimens should be wary of the hand and attempt to escape when touched. Do not select specimens that show no fight, flight, or fright.

Handling
Amphibians are not animals to be handled and petted at every opportunity. Not only is it bad for the animals, but many newts and salamanders secrete a toxic protective fluid from glands in the skin that can cause intense irritation to the mucous membranes. Their sensitive skins cannot tolerate the salt content and heat of a sweaty human hand. Salamanders and newts should therefore be handled as little as possible, and only when it is necessary for examination purposes. One such time is when purchasing new specimens from a dealer. The hands should be washed under running water to remove excess salt and left wet. The salamander or newt can be picked up by cupping the hand over the whole body and gently restraining it. The animal can then be examined by opening the fingers, but care should be taken that it does not fall. With aquatic specimens and larvae it is best to use a net to fish the animal out of the water; it can

be examined by manipulating the net. After handling amphibians, the hands should be washed again to remove any potentially dangerous toxins. Another thing to be borne in mind is that certain species of salamanders are unable to tolerate the poisons of others, so species should be kept separate if one is unsure of their interactions.

Transport
To avoid stress to the animals, they should be transported in the most humane way possible. Terrestrial salamanders are best placed in a plastic box with a secure lid. Damp sphagnum moss in the box serves two purposes: it prevents the animals becoming desiccated, and it acts as a shock absorber should the containers receive rough treatment. Adequate ventilation holes should be drilled in the box. The salamanders should be transported to their destination as quickly as possible. Boxes should not be allowed to chill in cold climates, and neither should they be exposed to the sun's rays. If several boxes are to be transported, they are best placed in an outer container lined with insulation material such as styrofoam.

Although newts and salamanders do not have a great number of diseases, it is still best to quarantine them for a couple of weeks before adding them to a community tank of any type. Notophthalmus viridescens.

Quarantine

Whenever new salamanders are acquired, it is considered essential that they undergo a period of quarantine before they are put in with existing stock. Many diseases can lie dormant in an animal, sometimes never causing any problem until the specimen becomes stressed. You may purchase an animal that looks perfectly healthy in every way, but it may be suffering the early stages of disease brought on by the trauma of recent capture and transportation. By placing a new animal in a special quarantine tank (with all the necessary life support systems but without elaborate decorations) for a minimum of 14 days, you can monitor its health without risking the welfare of your existing stock. After the prescribed time the salamander can be placed in its permanent home, providing no symptoms of disease have been observed.

General Hygiene

Good ventilation is the key to keeping terraria in good condition. Unfortunately, the enclosed humid environments provided for our salamanders also provide ideal conditions for bacteria, fungi, and other undesirables to multiply. By providing good ventilation in addition to high humidity, growth of certain organisms can be minimized. Garden soil is particularly subject to bacterial growth. It is best to use only materials that have been presterilized. It is also advisable to minimize tank decorations to the bare essentials. Washed gravel is best as a substrate. Any plants used can be potted, the pots being sunk into the gravel or hidden behind rocks.

When handling objects in a particular terrarium, always wash the hands thoroughly before going to the next one, even if there are no obvious signs of disease. This way you will ensure that you are not the culprit who spreads disease through the stock. Terraria will have to be routinely cleaned out at regular intervals or after an outbreak of disease. In the latter case, all contents of the tank should be destroyed by burning (plants, branches, etc.) or sterilized by boiling (rocks, gravel, water containers, etc.). Never use commercial disinfectants in a terrarium for salamanders; even the smallest amounts of residual chemicals can be stressful or even fatal. The only type of disinfectant recommended for use in cleaning terraria is a solution of sodium hypochlorite (household bleach). A 10% solution of this chemical will kill off even the most stubborn of bacteria in the terrarium and, providing the container and its contents are thoroughly rinsed with clean water, there is little danger from the residue.

Diseases

Salamanders kept in good

The slightly swollen and pustulate pores and lateral line organs of this spotted salamander, Ambystoma maculatum, *indicate that it might have a bacterial or viral disease.*

hygienic conditions with all their necessary life support systems working properly rarely succumb to disease. Indeed, most outbreaks of disease can usually be traced to some inadequacy in the husbandry. The following are problems that may occur from time to time.

Nutritional Disorders: As most salamanders and newts feed on a variety of invertebrates, nutritional disorders are only likely to occur where there is a lack of variety in the diet (when only mealworms are given as food, for example). Various mineral and vitamin deficiencies can cause symptoms such as deformed bone growth, malfunction of the nervous system, skin disorders, and eye troubles. Where it is not possible to feed a varied diet for part of the year, it is recommended that a suitable vitamin and mineral supplement be added to the diet.

Wounds: Open wounds that can become infected with bacteria are usually caused when nervous animals try to escape. Newly acquired animals should always be left in peace to settle into their new surroundings and should be disturbed as little as possible. Once accustomed to their terrarium, injury is less likely.

For the prevention of bacterial infection of wounds and the promotion of healing, an antibiotic powder may be applied. It is best to obtain advice from a veterinarian before attempting to use complex chemicals on salamanders.

Fungal Infections: Aquatic species are particularly susceptible to fungal infections of the type sometimes seen in fishes. Such infections manifest themselves as areas of inflamed skin surrounded by whitish tissue. Untreated, this can be fatal. Infected animals should be immersed in a 2% solution of malachite green or Mercurochrome for five minutes. This should be repeated at daily intervals until a cure is effected. If no improvement is shown after seven days, a veterinarian who knows amphibians should be consulted.

Hibernation

Salamanders from colder climates hibernate during the winter months either by burying themselves in mud at the bottom of ponds or by hiding in burrows deep enough to avoid the frost. During hibernation the animal's rate of metabolism is reduced to such an extent that it requires barely any oxygen, let alone food. This period of hibernation is an important part of the life cycle. Many species come into breeding condition, ready to mate, as the springtime temperatures and photoperiods wake them from their winter "sleep." Although it is possible to keep salamanders active and feeding all the year around in captivity by keeping the temperatures up, they are unlikely to breed and their lives may be shortened.

A period of simulated hibernation is enough to provide temperate species with all they require for a "normal" life cycle, including increased prospects of successful breeding. In the fall, reduce the temperature of the terrarium gradually over several days and stop feeding the animals. Remove the terrarium to a frost-free outbuilding where the temperature can be maintained at not less than 3°C (37°F) and preferably not more than 10°C (50°F). Alternatively, the salamanders can be packed in slightly damp sphagnum moss in plastic boxes and kept in the refrigerator for two to three months at 3°C (37°F).

Ensatina eschscholtzi occurs in cool coniferous forests of the United States West Coast. When the species is kept in captivity it must be given a winter rest period during which it can hibernate as it would in the wild.

THE AXOLOTL

Of the 350 or so species of living salamanders and newts, the axolotl has been chosen here to warrant a chapter all to itself. There are a number of reasons for this, the least of which is that the axolotl is probably the most commonly kept "pet" amphibian of all. It is also used widely in laboratories for biological studies and is often seen in the biology departments of schools and colleges. In its normal form the axolotl is totally aquatic. In most climates it can be kept in unheated aquaria in much the same conditions as one would keep cold-water fishes. The axolotl is particularly recommended for the beginner to salamander keeping as it is easy to care for, easy to replace should a disaster occur, and gives one an experience with and "feel" for this group of animals

Ambystoma mexicanum, *the axolotl. Recently this readily cultured salamander has become available in pet shops, and it now seems to be quite popular with keepers. Formerly it was cultured mostly for physiology experiments in college laboratories.*

Classification of the Axolotl

Class:	Amphibia
Order:	Caudata
Suborder:	Ambystomatoidea
Family:	Ambystomatidae
Genus:	*Ambystoma*
Species:	*Ambystoma mexicanum*

before advancing to more ambitious projects.

History

During the early 16th century, when Spanish conquistadors first arrived in what is today called Mexico, they were fascinated and sometimes amazed by the number of things that were totally alien to them. One of these things was the strange creature which the native Aztecs called *axolotl* (difficult to translate, but roughly meaning "water-beast" or "water-play"). This creature appeared to be both worshipped and used on the menu of peoples living near certain deep freshwater lakes, in particular Lake Xochimilcho, which is near the present day Mexico City. It took a long time for scientists to fully understand this "half-beast, half-fish," and it has been taxonomically reclassified several times. Superficially resembling a larval salamander, retaining its feathery gills and remaining aquatic throughout its life, its general appearance at first led herpetologists to classify it among the waterdogs and the sirens, salamanders that were known to have no terrestrial form. The famous German explorer Alexander von Humboldt collected specimens of the axolotl in 1803 and brought them to Europe, where they were examined by the renowned zoologist Cuvier. In his *Animal Kingdom*, first published in 1828, he declared that axolotls "altogether resemble the tadpole of the salamander." He did not, in fact, know how right he was. It was over 100 years later that the axolotl was finally placed correctly in the suborder Ambystomatoidea and given its present scientific name of *Ambystoma mexicanum*.

Description

At full size, a sexually mature axolotl reaches a length of 25 cm (10 in), although the average seems to be more like 20 cm (8 in). The wild (or normal) variety is dark brown in color with darker sooty brown to blackish blotches and spots. The underside is a shade lighter. In captivity albino (off-white) specimens with pink eyes are common, as are varieties with patches of dark and light colors. The axolotl has a broad,

Since axolotls have been bred for decades in laboratories, several mutations have appeared and been stabilized. The pied pattern is the most commonly seen color mutation, and even it comes in many shades of color. Pied animals make the most attractive pets.

streamlined head with a very wide mouth and a blunt snout. Oriented toward the top of the head is a pair of small lidless eyes. The rather small limbs are spaced well apart on the robust body, which possesses a series of vertical (costal) grooves along the flanks. The four fingers of the forelimbs and the five toes are webless or only negligibly webbed. A low crest starting just behind the head runs back and becomes higher on the tail, which is flattened from side to side. The crest is also developed on the underside of the tail and aids in the swimming action of the animal, which is accomplished by lateral undulations of the body and tail. The limbs are not used for swimming propulsion but may be used for steering and braking as well as for walking about on the substrate. A very obvious feature of the axolotl, one that usually rouses comment from those who see the creature for the first time, is the prominent pair of three-lobed feathery gills that project up to 2 cm (3/4 in) from the rear sides of the head. In normal specimens the gills are a deep reddish brown, but in albinos they are bright crimson.

On hatching, the larvae are less than 1 cm (3/8 in) in length and much lighter in color than the normal adults, but they darken as they increase in size. In the wild state, axolotls are not known to metamorphose into terrestrial forms, but in captivity they can be persuaded to change into typical adult salamanders by gradually reducing the water depth over a period of several months. The first discovery of such a metamorphosis took place at the Jardin des Plantes in Paris during 1865, when a number of axolotls that had been imported the previous year began to breed. The resulting offspring developed into full-sized larvae within six months. The staff were amazed when a number of these gradually absorbed their gills, lost their crests, and left the water as creatures closely resembling the tiger salamander (*Ambystoma tigrinum*) of North America. It was at first thought that the axolotl was the larva of this species! During the 1870's, experiments at the University of Freiburg in Germany further ascertained that the larvae would metamorphose if kept in shallow water, thus encouraging them to take atmospheric air. It was also discovered that the process could be halted at any stage almost up to full metamorphosis by again increasing the water depth, which would cause the partially absorbed gills to redevelop.

Research on the axolotl in more recent times has shown that metamorphosis is encouraged by the production of thyroxine in the thyroid gland. Axolotls will develop into terrestrial salamanders if injected with a small quantity of this hormone. The introduction of small quantities of iodine into the water in which the salamanders are kept has been found to promote production of thyroxine by the animals, also leading to complete metamorphosis. It can therefore be concluded that the axolotl is the neotenous larva of an ambystomid salamander that does not metamorphose in the natural state. Neoteny is the persistence in an animal of larval features throughout its normal life, yet the animal is able to reproduce while in this state. Reproduction in such animals is known as pedogenesis.

Another outstanding property of the axolotl (shared with many other salamanders) is its ability to regenerate parts of its anatomy. Being naturally voracious, a hungry axolotl will have no qualms about biting off a limb or gill from one of its companions. Within a few weeks a new and almost perfect appendage will grow to replace the missing one. In the case of a limb, this is usually complete and with the correct number of digits, although it is not rare for one or two extra fingers or toes to be observed!

Housing

Axolotls can be kept in most kinds of aquaria, but overcrowding should be avoided. As a general rule, allow one adult axolotl to each 450 sq cm (72 sq in) of water surface area. A 60 cm long by 30 cm wide (2 ft × 1 ft) aquarium will therefore be suitable for not more than four specimens.

A fairly coarse shingle (approximately pea-sized) is the best kind of floor covering to use in the tank. Large, smooth pebbles used as background decoration will set the animals off most attractively. For maximum effect, use dark decoration materials for albino axolotls and light ones for dark specimens. To minimize squabbling and possible injury, the salamanders should be provided with a number of caves where weaker specimens can take refuge should the going get tough. Planting is usually futile, as the axolotls will soon grub out the roots in their quest for food. If planting is contemplated in large tanks, only robust plants should be used and these should be allowed to establish a substantial root system before the axolotls are introduced.

For normal purposes, the water should be 30 cm (1 ft) or more in depth. Supplementary heating is unnecessary unless the animals are kept in very cold climates. The axolotl will tolerate a wide range of temperatures, although it seems to do best in the region of 17–20°C (63–68°F), which is easy to maintain in the average home. Water filtration is essential, and it would be wise to install a power filter and perhaps an undergravel filter if you want to avoid cleaning out the tank at frequent intervals and unnecessarily stressing the animals. Information on the various kinds of filters available can be obtained

White axolotls are also common. All the color varieties can be kept just like the basic brownish mottled animal.

from your local pet shop, and the proprietor will be only too pleased to advise what he considers the best kind of system for your individual purposes. The filters should remove all of the suspended particles left over from feeding and defecation. (Axolotls are quite "dirty" animals.) Larger portions of foul matter, food leftovers, and pieces of dead vegetation should be removed daily using a siphon, otherwise the water will quickly become fouled.

Supplementary lighting is not essential to axolotls. The light from windows should be adequate, but the tank should not be placed in direct sunlight or overheating may result. Sunlight may also cause a buildup of green algae on the aquarium glass. If plants are to be cultured in the tank, it will be necessary to have a couple of fluorescent light tubes of the type recommended for horticultural use. Such lights also enhance the colors of the animals, showing them off nicely. Adequate aeration is essential, so an air pump should be used if filters are not installed.

Feeding

Being carnivorous, axolotls in the wild state will devour almost any living creature they can overpower. They are extremely voracious, and it is not unknown for them to tackle prey larger than themselves, although in this case they usually are not successful. Large axolotls will also eat smaller specimens, so be sure to keep animals of a similar size together. Provided they receive adequate food they are unlikely to attack each other, but on the rare occasions when one sees fit to bite the limb or gill from another, there is no need for undue worry. The injured animal should be moved to an isolation tank, where it will soon grow a new appendage to replace the one bitten off.

Axolotls are very easy to feed in captivity. In spite of the fact that raw meat is readily taken, this alone does not constitute a balanced diet. It must be supplemented with various livefoods to provide the additional vitamins, minerals, and roughage. In the absence of livefood for any lengthy period of time, it is recommended that a good quality vitamin and mineral supplement powder be worked into the meat before it is fed to the axolotls. Never feed more than will be eaten at one feeding or the water will soon become polluted.

Earthworms of most kinds

A female axolotl with part of its egg mass. Usually over 100 eggs are laid, and most of them will hatch. Obviously you need a lot of room to raise the larvae.

are eagerly taken, as are water snails, small land snails, slugs, mealworms, and many other insects. Very small axolotls, particularly the newly hatched juveniles, are more difficult to feed. One must arrange for a steady supply of livefood of suitable size, such as water fleas, mosquito larvae, brine shrimp, whiteworms, tubifex, and similar organisms, which are suitable for feeding axolotls of various sizes.

Breeding
In the early days, axolotl breeding was rather a hit and miss affair and occurred

These fully developed larvae are at the stage when they will escape from the egg membrane and begin to fend for themselves. They do not have to be fed for two days after hatching because they still have yolk reserves.

more by luck than by plan, until it was discovered that thermal shock would bring the animals into breeding condition. Large axolotls of both sexes that were apparently sexually mature were kept together for months, even years, with no sign of reproductive activity. However, it was found that if a few cubes of ice were added to the water, enough to reduce the normal temperature to about 10°C (50°F), courtship would commence almost immediately. A probable explanation for this phenomenon is that in the wild, the axolotl is triggered into springtime breeding activity by the seasonally melting snows from the surrounding mountains, which would temporarily reduce the water temperature of the lake habitat.

Adults of both sexes are similar in size and shape, the only obvious distinction being the marked swelling around the cloaca (vent) in the mature male. After selecting a suitable mate, the male axolotl will court her by making stylized movements of his body, which includes bending almost double, and rapid movements of the tail. Finally he will deposit a spermatophore on the substrate close to the female. If receptive, she will position herself over the sperm packet and take it into her cloaca, where it will be available to fertilize the eggs as they are laid. Oviposition occurs within 48 hours of mating. The female will seek out suitable water plants on which to deposit the eggs. Grasping a leaf with her hind limbs and pressing her vent against a leaf, she will deposit a small packet of eggs that will adhere to the plant. Such egglaying is often accompanied by violent body contortions. The process may be repeated several times over a period of hours. An excess of 100 eggs is usually laid.

After oviposition, the parent axolotls will show no further interest in the eggs other than as the source of an easy meal. Even if they did not eat the eggs, they would almost certainly devour the hatchlings. It is therefore a requirement to remove the eggs to a separate container for hatching and rearing. It is quite easy to spot the eggs by looking carefully among the water plants in the tank. They are about 2 mm (1/12 in) in diameter, with an obvious dark nucleus. It is best to cut the egg-bearing stems from the plants rather than to risk damage by handling them individually. The eggs are placed in shallow trays of water about 5 cm (2 in) deep. This water should be fresh, chlorine-free, well aerated, and kept at an average temperature of 20°C (68°F) for the period of incubation, which usually is about 14 days. Any eggs that turn milky white in color are infertile and should be removed with a pipette before they decay and pollute the water. The head, tail, and gill development of the embryos can be discerned after five days.

On hatching, the tiny axolotls will remain in close proximity to the egg case, still absorbing nourishment from the yolk. It is unnecessary to feed them for 48 hours, after which they may be given infusoria, brine shrimp, and/or water fleas. Pounded lean meat and hard-boiled egg yolk may also be given, but in extremely conservative quantities to avoid water pollution. The larvae soon become active, and at five days of age they may be moved with a fine-meshed net into a container of deeper,

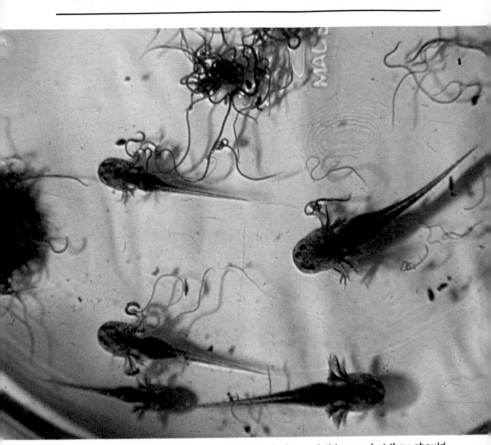

Tubifex worms are one of the standard foods for axolotl larvae, but they should never be the only food. All commonly kept newts and salamanders must have varied diets, even as larvae.

well-aerated water and kept at room temperature. Well-fed youngsters grow rapidly and will soon be able to tackle larger prey items, including tubifex, whiteworms, mosquito larvae, and small earthworms. Axolotls that are properly cared for will reach maturity in as little as six months and may breed at this age, but it is best to wait until they are nine months to a year old for best results. At regular intervals a certain amount of thinning out and size grading should be carried out in order to avoid overcrowding and possible cannibalism. Larger specimens will eat the smaller ones if you are not careful. Excess specimens may be sold or given away to fellow enthusiasts.

SELECTED SALAMANDERS AND NEWTS

With over 350 species of salamanders and newts known to science, it would be impossible to describe more than a few of them in a volume of this size. Therefore, the author has attempted to assemble a list of better-known species from various families, most of which will breed in captivity given the correct conditions. In addition, a few more "difficult" species have been added to whet the appetite of those who, having gained experience with the more common types, wish to advance onto more ambitious projects. The emphasis has been on aquatic and semiaquatic species as they are more readily obtained and usually easier to care for. American woodland salamanders (Plethodontidae) have been slighted, but few species of this family are available commercially or make good pets.

Salamanders and newts may be obtained from dealers who specialize in reptiles and amphibians, from enthusiasts already in the process of regular captive breeding, or you may collect specimens from the wild. Before taking this latter course it is advisable to make yourself aware of national and local legislation concerning the protection and collection of wildlife. Some species may be protected in various areas (such as national parks); others may have protected status in certain states or countries. It can be a serious offense to interfere with protected species in the wild, so beware!

In the following text, the lengths given are the maximum size to which one may expect an adult to grow; in most cases they are likely to mature somewhat smaller.

Hellbender

Cryptobranchus alleganiensis
Family: Cryptobranchidae
Length: 76 cm (30 in)

DESCRIPTION: The hellbender belongs to a family of salamanders containing only three species. The other two are the giant salamanders of the genus *Andrias* from China and Japan, which are virtually unobtainable to the enthusiast due to their protected status. The hellbender is a large, totally aquatic salamander with a flattened head and body; along the lower flanks is a loose flap of skin. It has a single pair of gill openings just behind the head, but no feathery external gills as seen in many aquatic species. The color is gray-brown above, often with darker mottling. The underside is lighter and without mottling. The male is somewhat smaller than the female. It has moderately large limbs with four fingers and five toes.

NATURAL RANGE: Central and eastern United States.

HABITAT AND HABITS: Found in fast-flowing streams and rivers, especially those with rocky bottoms. The animals usually hide beneath submerged rocks or logs or in cavities in the river bank, coming out at night to search for food.

CAPTIVE CARE: Suited only to very large, well aerated aquaria with gravel substrate and large rock caves for hiding places. Room temperature is adequate. Provision should be made for a reduction of temperature in the winter. Will feed on a variety of vertebrate and invertebrate food including strips of lean raw meat, small fishes, crayfishes, and earthworms.

BREEDING: Little documentation is available on the captive breeding of this species. In the wild, the male excavates a nest cavity usually below a large flat rock. The female lays 200-500 yellowish eggs in long strings that are fertilized by the male and pushed into the nest cavity. The male guards the nest for the period of incubation.

Siberian Salamander
Hynobius keyserlingii
Family: Hynobiidae
Length: 13 cm (5¼ in)

DESCRIPTION: This is the most well-known member of the primitive Asian family Hynobiidae, which contains some 30 species in five genera. *Hynobius* has relatively large limbs with four fingers and only a rudimentary fifth toe. The body is robust and typically "salamander shaped," running into a round

The terrestrial eft of the red-spotted newt, Notophthalmus viridescens, *is one of the most attractive North American salamanders. It can be kept like other small terrestrial species but must be allowed to change to the aquatic form when ready.*

tail flattened at its tip. The upper side is olive-brown with a black dorsal stripe bordered by a gold-bronze shimmering line. The flanks are marbled with black or dark brown, and the lower sides may be covered with tiny white spots. The underside is lighter in color.

NATURAL RANGE: Siberia and a small area west of the Urals.

HABITAT AND HABITS: Inhabits marshy and semi-woodland areas never far from the breeding waters. Mainly nocturnal, it hides during the day in mossy clumps or among tree roots.

CAPTIVE CARE: Provide a medium sized aqua-terrarium, unheated and planted with moss and grass clumps. Food should consist of a variety of small invertebrates. It is recommended that this species be hibernated for at least three months during the winter. Alternatively, this species may be kept in an outdoor enclosure.

BREEDING: After fertilization, the female lays her eggs in a sort of capsule that is suspended in vegetation near to the water's edge, just touching the surface film. Mating activity occurs very early in the spring and has been observed at 3°C (37°F). The larvae hatch in about 14 days and drop into the water, where they develop in the normal manner.

Fire Salamander

Salamandra salamandra
Family: Salamandridae
Length: 28 cm (11 in)

DESCRIPTION: The family Salamandridae contains some 43 species in 15 genera and is distributed through North America, Eurasia, and North Africa. The European fire salamander was one of the first in the family to be described and is the subject of many legends and fables. *S. salamandra* is a truly handsome beast, its glossy black body being marked with bright yellow or orange blotches, stripes, or spots, depending on which of the many subspecies is being described.

NATURAL RANGE: Western, central, and southern Europe, northwestern Africa, and parts of southwestern Asia.

HABITAT AND HABITS: Found mainly in woodlands and heavily forested areas, usually in hilly or mountainous country, although a few populations occur at suitable lower altitudes. It lives in damp situations, rarely far from water, and hides during the day under or within rotting timber. It is primarily nocturnal and comes out at night to hunt terrestrial invertebrates. Its bright colors warn potential predators of its noxious skin secretions that can severely irritate the mucous membranes of predators.

CAPTIVE CARE: A large aqua-terrarium with adequate hiding places consisting of mossy clumps and pieces of dead bark. A few woodland plants may be added for decoration. Supplementary heating is unnecessary in most situations. It is recommended that captive specimens be allowed to undergo a period of hibernation. Feed on a variety of invertebrates.

BREEDING: This species gives birth to well-developed larvae or even fully developed young. Captive breeding success is most likely to occur in outdoor enclosures.

Alpine Salamander

Salamandra atra
Family: Salamandridae
Length: 16 cm (6¼ in)

DESCRIPTION: Although similar to S. salamandra in shape, S. atra is smaller and glossy black in color. Occasionally dark brown or even albino specimens are found. There is a prominent parotid gland situated on either side of the neck.

NATURAL RANGE: Found only in the European Alps and in the mountainous regions of western Yugoslavia and northern Albania.

HABITAT AND HABITS: Occurs naturally only in mountainous areas, usually at altitudes between 500 and 3000 m (1600–9700 ft). Mainly found in woodland habitats, but occasionally in alpine meadows. It is mainly nocturnal and hides during the day under logs or stones; it may be seen abroad in the daylight after heavy summer rains.

CAPTIVE CARE: A difficult species that should not be kept unless the correct conditions can be provided. A medium sized terrarium is required. A water vessel is unnecessary. The temperature should never be allowed above 20°C (68°F), and the humidity must be kept high but without excessive free water. The substrate may consist of gravel covered with sterilized loam planted with mosses and ferns. A few flat stones should be provided for hiding places. Winter hibernation at a temperature just above 0°C (32°F) is essential if reproduction is to be accomplished. Feeds on a variety of small invertebrates.

BREEDING: Mating occurs shortly after hibernation and courtship is similar to that of S. salamandra. However, free water is not required for the larvae as complete metamorphosis occurs within the maternal body, the mother depositing usually two but up to four small but perfect replicas of their parents.

Spectacled Salamander

Salamandrina terdigitata
Family: Salamandridae
Length: 11 cm (4½ in)

DESCRIPTION: This is the only European salamander with four fingers *and* four toes. It is a small, slender species with a rather long head and prominent eyes. The long tail is cylindrical, with a prominent dorsal ridge. The upper side is bronze-brown to black. There is a lighter area around the eyes that gives it its common name. The underside is pale with a dark throat and blotches on the belly. In adults the undersides of the limbs and part of the tail are a bright fiery red.

NATURAL RANGE: Restricted to the western half of the Italian peninsula.

HABITAT AND HABITS: Usually confined to forested mountain slopes with thick undergrowth, rarely far from mountain streams. It lives among rocks

Onychodactylus fischeri is an uncommonly seen northern Asian salamander. It must be kept cool and allowed access to moisture. The hynobiid salamanders are rarely kept as pets.

and ground debris. Mainly nocturnal, but may appear after heavy rain during the summer. When threatened, it will curl up its tail to expose the bright red underside. With the exception of the spring breeding season, this species is wholly terrestrial.

CAPTIVE CARE: A large aqua-terrarium with the land area greater than that of the water, which should be kept clean and well aerated. The substrate should consist of gravel and sterilized loam in which moss and ferns can be planted. A few pieces of bark and flat stones can be provided as hiding places. Feed on a variety of small invertebrates. The terrarium atmosphere should be humid but not wet. A summer temperature of 22°C (72°F) should be maintained, reduced to 10–15°C (50–59°F) during the winter.

BREEDING: Courtship and fertilization occur on land in much the same manner as in *S. salamandra*. The female enters the water to lay usually 30–90 eggs that are affixed to water plants and pebbles in groups of

73

6–12. Full metamorphosis occurs in about eight weeks, at which time the young salamanders will begin a terrestrial existence.

Golden-striped Salamander
Chioglossa lusitanica
Family: Salamandridae
Length: 15 cm (6 in)

DESCRIPTION: A relatively long, slender species with distinct costal grooves along the flanks. The upper side is brown with two copper or gold colored stripes along the back that join at the base of the tail and continue as a single stripe.

NATURAL RANGE: Confined to the northern half of Portugal and northwestern Spain.

HABITAT AND HABITS: Mainly nocturnal, this species spends the daylight hours hiding under stones and vegetation in wet mountain areas. It can move rapidly and scuttles for cover in a lizard-like manner when disturbed. Also like some lizards, it can shed its tail as a protective measure.

CAPTIVE CARE: An aqua-terrarium with roughly one-third water and two-thirds land. The latter can be planted with moss

The hellbender, Cryptobranchus alleganiensis, *is one of the most primitive sala-manders. It is also totally aquatic, very large, and needs a large, cool aquarium.*

and ferns. Hiding places should be provided in the shape of bark and flat stones. Summer temperatures 15–22°C (59–72°F), reduced to just above 0°C (32°F) for hibernation. This species also requires a period of summer estivation when the humidity may be reduced. Feed on a variety of small invertebrates.

BREEDING: Courtship and egg-laying are similar to that described for *Salamandrina terdigitata*.

Pyrenean Brook Salamander
Euproctus asper
Family: Salamandridae
Length: 16 cm (6½ in)

DESCRIPTION: A relatively robust species with a flattened body. There are no apparent paratoid glands. The skin is rough and colored grayish brown or olive with yellowish markings, these sometimes forming an indistinct vertebral stripe. Dark bordered light blotches occur along the flanks. The underside is usually yellow or light orange with darker flecks.

NATURAL RANGE: Occurs only in the eastern three-quarters of the Pyrenees. Closely related species include the Corsican brook salamander, *E. montanus* and the Sardinian brook salamander, *E. platycephalus*.

HABITAT AND HABITS: Fairly aquatic and never far from water at altitudes of 700–2500 meters (approx. 2000–8000 ft). Mainly nocturnal, usually hiding during the day under stones or in cavities near the water's edge.

CAPTIVE CARE: Should only be kept where water temperatures can be maintained at 18°C (65°F) and below. An aquarium with well aerated shallow water is required, with a few landing sites consisting of mossy rocks or tree roots. Clean gravel should be used for the substrate. It is important that the water is kept crystal-clear (a filter is essential). The temperature should be reduced to around 5°C (41°F) in the winter. Feeds on a variety of small invertebrates.

BREEDING: Courtship takes place in the water in early spring. The male takes hold of the female with his muscular tail and one of his hind limbs, stroking the female's cloaca with his free hind leg. The spermatophore is immediately taken up by the female in her cloaca. The eggs are laid singly in gaps and cavities in the stony substrate.

Sharp-ribbed Newt; Rough Newt
Pleurodeles waltl
Family: Salamandridae
Length: 30 cm (12 in)

DESCRIPTION: Perhaps the largest of the European salamanders, although few specimens reach the maximum length of 30 cm (12 in). A row of warty tubercles along the flanks coincides with the tips of the sharp ribs that sometimes actually project through the skin. The broad head is very flat and the heavy body is rough-skinned. The upper side is olive to grayish yellow with dark brown blotches; older animals are usually darker in color. The warts along the flanks may be yellow or orange, while the underside may be

European fire salamanders, Salamandra salamandrå, *are strikingly colored, not uncommonly available, and often bred in captivity.*

yellow, off-white or gray, usually with darker blotches. Breeding males have dark, rough patches on the inner sides of their forelimbs.

NATURAL RANGE: The Iberian peninsula with the exception of the north and northeast; Morocco.

HABITAT AND HABITS: Mainly aquatic when conditions are suitable, but is forced to become terrestrial when water courses dry up. Mainly nocturnal, living in slow-moving waters including ponds, ditches, shallow lakes, and cisterns.

CAPTIVE CARE: Requires a large aquarium with an island. The water should be 20–25 cm (8–10 in) deep. Floating water plants can be installed to allow the salamanders to rest at the water surface while taking air. Rooted plants will simply be pulled out of the substrate by the active animals. They feed on larger invertebrates such as earthworms, mealworms and locusts; raw strips of lean meat may also be given. Maintain at 25°C (77°F) in the summer and reduce to around 8°C (46°F) for the winter rest period.

BREEDING: Courtship occurs in the water. The male positions himself under the female, presses his head against her throat, and makes rubbing motions. He then takes hold of one of her forelimbs with his. Often he will stay in this position for many hours, even days, while the female transports him about. Eventually a spermatophore is deposited by the male and it is immediately taken up by the female. The eggs, which may number up to 1000, are laid In clumps on water plants or stones.

Breeding male Triturus cristatus, *the European crested newt, are striking salamanders.*

The belly of the adult crested newt is bright yellow in some populations, accented by black spots

Great Crested or Warty Newt
Triturus cristatus
Family: Salamandridae
Length: 18 cm (7 in)

DESCRIPTION: A robust species with a black, warty skin. During the aquatic breeding season the male takes on a special courtship dress that includes a high, toothed crest along the spine, running into the tail. At this time he develops a series of tiny white spots along the flanks and a light blue flash on the flattened tail. The limbs are of moderate size, with four fingers and five toes. Both male and

Three European newts: Top: Euproctus montanus, *the Corsican brook salamander;* Center: Triturus vulgaris, *the common newt;* Bottom: Triturus marmoratus, *the marbled newt.*

female possess a black-spotted red or orange color on the belly throughout the year.

NATURAL RANGE: Found in most parts of Europe but absent from southwestern France, the Iberian peninsula, southern Greece, and the Mediterranean islands. It also extends into central Asia.

HABITAT AND HABITS: Usually found near still water and particularly common in agricultural districts with alkaline soil. In some parts of its range it may remain aquatic throughout the year; in others it leaves the water after the breeding season

and is nocturnal and secretive, hiding during the day under logs and stones or in cavities in the ground.

CAPTIVE CARE: Should be kept in an unheated aqua-terrarium with a good water depth. The water should be planted with robust pond weeds such as *Elodea.* The land area can have a turf covering and one or two prostrate woodland plants.

BREEDING: Covered in detail earlier. Success is most likely to occur in suitable outdoor enclosures.

Marbled Newt

Triturus marmoratus
Family: Salamandridae
Length: 16 cm (6¼ in)

DESCRIPTION: This species is easily distinguished from other European newts by its beautiful green coloring that is marbled with brown and black. The belly is pale, and there is a yellow dorsal stripe. The male develops an untoothed dorsal crest in the breeding season.

NATURAL RANGE: This species replaces *T. cristatus* in southwestern France and the Iberian peninsula.

HABITAT AND HABITS: If anything, the marbled newt is less aquatic than *T. cristatus* and spends most of the year on land, sometimes in relatively dry surroundings. It is commonly found at lower altitudes than its cousin.

CAPTIVE CARE: A large aqua-terrarium is required, with the land area relatively dry. During spring, summer, and fall the temperature should be maintained at 20–25°C (68–77°F), with a reduction to 10°C (50°F) during the winter rest period.

BREEDING: It is possible to breed this species in large, well-planted aquaria when the newts come into breeding condition in the spring. The water temperature should be gradually increased to 25°C (77°F) and maintained until the larvae metamorphose. Natural hybridization with *T. cristatus* is known to occur where the ranges overlap, and this has also been accomplished in captive conditions. A combination of the green marbling of the marbled newt and the red underside of the warty newt produces an animal of great beauty.

Smooth Newt

Triturus vulgaris
Family: Salamandridae
Length: 10 cm (4 in)

DESCRIPTION: Outside the breeding season this small species is a dull olive color with a light orange underside. In breeding condition, however, the male develops a high, continuous wavy crest, large black blotches develop on the body, and the orange color of the belly intensifies. There may be a bluish flash along the lower margin of the tail.

NATURAL RANGE: A common species found over much of Europe and into Asia, but absent from the Iberian peninsula and the southern half of Italy.

HABITAT AND HABITS: Terrestrial outside the breeding season, it is secretive and nocturnal, hiding under logs and debris during the day. Found in damp situations rarely far from the breeding ponds.

CAPTIVE CARE: A medium-sized, unheated aqua-terrarium is required. The temperature should not exceed 22°C (72°F). Aquatic and terrestrial plants can be used for decoration, and hiding places can be provided in the form of pieces of bark, flat stones, or broken flowerpots. Food consists of a variety of small invertebrates.

BREEDING: May be bred in a planted aquarium or in an outdoor pond. A large supply of tiny aquatic invertebrates is necessary for the rearing of the larvae.

Palmate Newt
Triturus helveticus
Family: Salamandridae
Length: 9 cm (3½ in)

DESCRIPTION: Similar in appearance to *T. vulgaris* but smaller and more slenderly built. The red color on the belly is replaced by silver or very pale yellow and the spots are relatively smaller. The breeding male develops a crest on the tail only; this is marked by a central orange stripe bordered with black spots. A good identification mark is the black filament at the tip of the male's tail.

NATURAL RANGE: Found in the western half of Europe, including England, Scotland, and Wales, but absent from Ireland, southern Iberia, and Scandinavia.

HABITAT AND HABITS: Usually more aquatic than *T. vulgaris*, this species breeds in a variety of small waters, including ponds, puddles, and heathland marshes. Found mainly in areas of acid soil. Becomes terrestrial in late summer and winter, when it is secretive and nocturnal.

CAPTIVE CARE: Should be kept in a medium sized aquaterrarium with peat in the substrate to encourage acidity. The substrate may be planted with aquatic and terrestrial plants and provided with a number of hiding places. Feeds on a variety of small invertebrates.

BREEDING: As for *T. vulgaris*.

Alpine Newt
Triturus alpestris
Family: Salamandridae
Length: 10 cm (4 in)

DESCRIPTION: This is a small but very attractive newt in which the male is very slender and smaller than the more robust female. In the terrestrial stage the dorsal surface is a dark brown to black, while the unmarked belly is bright orange. The breeding male develops a low crest with

The palmate newt, Triturus helveticus.

The bright orange belly of this alpine newt, Triturus alpestris, is one of its most distinctive features.

alternating white and dark vertical bars. Both sexes develop a blue stripe marked with small dark spots along the flanks.

NATURAL RANGE: Central Europe from the western coasts of France and the Netherlands east into Russia and the Balkans and south into northern Italy. An isolated population exists in northern Spain.

HABITAT AND HABITS: A very aquatic species never found far from water. It inhabits damp woodlands at high altitudes, particularly in the southern part of its range. In its terrestrial stage it is usually found in damp, mossy environments.

CAPTIVE CARE: A medium sized aqua-terrarium with temperature not exceeding 20°C (68°F). The land area should be planted with mossy clumps. Pieces of rotting timber will provide hiding places.

Feeds on a variety of small invertebrates.

BREEDING: As for *T. vulgaris*. Success is most likely to occur in suitable outdoor enclosures.

Italian Newt

Triturus italicus
Family: Salamandridae
Length: 7.5 cm (3 in)

DESCRIPTION: This tiny species is Europe's smallest newt. Apart from its size, it is similar to *T. vulgaris* although lighter in color and often more heavily mottled.

NATURAL RANGE: Restricted to southern Italy.

HABITAT AND HABITS: In its terrestrial stage it lives secretively in damp situations like other newts. During the breeding season it inhabits small, still waters such as pools and cisterns.

CAPTIVE CARE: A small to

medium sized aqua-terrarium with summer temperatures to 26°C (79°F). Hibernation is unnecessary, but a temperature reduction to 15°C (59°F) in the winter is recommended. Feeds on a variety of very small invertebrates.

BREEDING: As recommended for *T. vulgaris*. Will successfully breed outdoors only in warmer areas or in greenhouses.

Japanese Fire-bellied Newt

Cynops pyrrhogaster
Family: Salamandridae
Length: 10 cm (4 in)

DESCRIPTION: Similar in size and shape to *T. vulgaris*. It is chocolate brown to black above and bright orange or red beneath. It has prominent parotid glands and dorso-lateral ridges. In the breeding season the male's tail takes on a bluish or purplish sheen.

NATURAL RANGE: Japan.

HABITAT AND HABITS: Fairly aquatic, it lives in vegetated ponds for most of the year. May be active both by day and at night.

CAPTIVE CARE: Requires an aquarium with a water depth of about 20 cm (8 in) and land areas consisting of mossy rocks breaking the surface. Alternatively, an aqua-terrarium with a land/water ratio of 1:2 can be used. The water area should be planted with aquatic species. The water should be filtered and maintained at around 20°C (68°F) in the summer but reduced to 5°C (41°F) for the winter rest period. Feeds on a variety of small invertebrates.

BREEDING: Courtship and mating take place in the spring in water. The eggs are laid on the leaves of water plants.

Red-spotted Newt

Notophthalmus viridescens
Family: Salamandridae
Length: 12 cm (5 in)

DESCRIPTION: One of the best known North American newts, this species is noted for the remarkable difference in appearance between aquatic adults and the juvenile terrestrial stage known as red efts. Adults are slender, smooth, yellowish-brown to olive above and yellowish below, with a sprinkling all over of dark spots. A number of dark bordered red spots are present on each side of the body. Red efts are dark, reddish brown to orange, with spots of lighter red along the flanks; their skin texture is very rough.

NATURAL RANGE: Southern part of eastern Canada and eastern half of the U.S.A.

HABITAT AND HABITS: Adults are mainly aquatic, living in shallow, heavily vegetated waters. They consume a variety of aquatic invertebrates and fish eggs, actively seeking out the spawning sites. Upon metamorphosis, the juvenile or red eft becomes terrestrial, living in leaf litter and undergrowth in damp, wooded areas and feeding upon small terrestrial invertebrates.

CAPTIVE CARE: Terraria should reflect the life-style of this species. A large aqua-terrarium will support both aquatic and land-dwelling forms and provide a breeding area for red efts when they reach maturity. Unheated terraria or aquaria are required, with the temperature not exceeding 22°C (72°F) in the summer. The temperature should be reduced to around 5°C (41°F) for the winter rest period.

BREEDING: Courtship occurs in the water in much the manner of European newts. The 200–400 eggs are laid singly on aquatic vegetation. These hatch in three to eight weeks into aquatic gilled larvae that metamorphose in the fall to spend the early part of their lives on land. The life history shows a great deal of variation with locality, some populations lacking the eft stage entirely. Efts may live on land for several years before returning to the water.

California Newt
Taricha torosa
Family: Salamandridae
Length: 18 cm (7 in)

DESCRIPTION: This species and its close relatives, the rough-skinned newt, *Taricha granulosa*, and the red-bellied newt, *T. rivularis*, are very similar in appearance. *T. torosa* is a fairly robust species with a roughly textured skin. It is tan to reddish brown above and orange to yellow below. The lower eyelid is pale and the eyes are large. In breeding males the skin becomes smooth, the tail becomes compressed, and horny tubercles develop on the toes.

NATURAL RANGE: Coastal California and the Sierras of California.

Japanese fire-bellied newts, Cynops pyrrhogaster, *are hardy and very colorful.*

Paramesotriton hongkongensis, *the Hong Kong newt, is a fairly commonly available species in American pet shops. Like other Asian newts, it requires fairly cool water.*

HABITAT AND HABITS: Mainly nocturnal, but may be seen abroad after heavy rain in damp areas. During dry periods it will estivate under forest debris and in the burrows of other animals. Mainly terrestrial, entering water only in the breeding season.

The red-spotted newt, Notophthalmus viridescens, *was once known as* Diemictylus.

CAPTIVE CARE: Requires a large aqua-terrarium with a planted land area. Maintain a temperature of around 22°C (72°F) in the summer. This should be reduced to about 10°C (50°F) for two or three months in the winter.

BREEDING: Breeds in the water from December to May. Courtship is similar to other newts. Eggs are laid on submersed plants. Larvae may metamorphose during the first season or in the following spring.

Two-toed Amphiuma
Amphiuma means
Family: Amphiumidae
Length: 100 cm (39 in)

DESCRIPTION: The Amphiumidae is the smallest salamander family, with only three species in a single genus. *A. means* is probably the best known. The other two species are *A. pholeter*, the one-toed amphiuma, and *A. tridactylum*, the three-toed amphiuma. *A. means* is a robust, eel-like salamander with four tiny limbs each with only two toes. There are no eyelids, and the eyes are very small. There are small gill openings just in front of the forelimbs but no external gills. The color is a uniform dark gray to brown above blending into a dark gray belly.

NATURAL RANGE: Southeastern coastal plain of the U.S.A. from southeastern Virginia through to Mississippi.

HABITAT AND HABITS: Totally aquatic, preferring acidic, vegetated, muddy waters, including swamps, bayous, and ditches. Nocturnal, hiding in its own submerged burrows or those of other aquatic animals such as crayfishes during the day. In wet weather it may migrate overland. In the wild it feeds on crayfishes, frogs, other salamanders, fishes, and even small water snakes.

CAPTIVE CARE: Requires a large well-aerated aquarium with a gravel substrate and larger rocks for hiding places. Aquatic plants are usually uprooted by the animals, so only floating plants should be used. Other decorations can include tree roots. The temperature of the water should be maintained at around 25°C (77°F) with a slight reduction in the winter. Feeds on large invertebrates, frogs, and strips of lean meat.

BREEDING: After courtship and mating in shallow water, the female lays a string of up to 200 eggs in a damp cavity near the water's edge, often under a flat stone or a log. The female remains protectively coiled around the eggs until they hatch, which may take up to five months. The larvae are about 5 cm (2 in) long and have pale gills.

In this subspecies of the red-spotted newt, N. v. dorsalis, the red spots are actually a broken red line.

Red efts of the red-spotted newt are very hardy for their size.

Mudpuppy
Necturus maculosus
Family: Proteidae
Length: 43 cm (17 in)

DESCRIPTION: The family Proteidae contains two genera, *Necturus* from North America with four or five species and *Proteus* with a single European species, the olm, *Proteus anguinus*. The mudpuppy is the best known of the North

American proteids. It is a large aquatic salamander with feathery dark red gills and four fingers and four toes. The body is robust, the tail compressed. The body is gray-brown to dark gray above, with dark edged bluish blotches. The underside is usually gray with darker spots.

NATURAL RANGE: Central and eastern North America.

HABITAT AND HABITS: Found in a variety of water bodies ranging from clear, fast-running streams to slow, muddy rivers. Those from well-oxygenated waters have short gills, while those from muddy, warm waters have large, bushy appendages. Mainly nocturnal and totally aquatic, it feeds upon a wide variety of aquatic invertebrates and small fishes.

CAPTIVE CARE: Requires a large aquarium with a water depth of at least 30 cm (12 in). The water should be aerated and filtered. Plants are usually a waste of time as the active animals will uproot them. Use a substrate of medium gravel and decorations of rocks and tree roots. They feed on various aquatic invertebrates and strips of lean meat or fish. Prefers a temperature of 22°C (72°F) in summer, reduced to around 5°C (41°F) in winter.

BREEDING: Fertilization is internal by spermatophores. The female lays 30-200 eggs during April to June. The eggs are laid singly and attached to the underside of rocks or debris. The larvae hatch in four to ten weeks. It takes four to six years for them to reach maturity.

Spotted Salamander
Ambystoma maculatum
Family: Ambystomatidae
Length: 25 cm (10 in)

DESCRIPTION: The family Ambystomatidae contains about 30 species in four genera found only in North America. The axolotl, *Ambystoma mexicanum*, is probably the best known and most commonly kept species, but other members of the family make interesting terrarium inmates. *A. maculatum* is a robust species with well developed limbs exhibiting four fingers and five toes. The basic color is black to blue-gray above with two irregular rows of large yellow or orange spots starting on the top of the head and extending to the tip of the tail. The belly is usually a plain slate-gray color.

NATURAL RANGE: Eastern North America from the Great Lakes and Nova Scotia almost to the Gulf Coast.

HABITAT AND HABITS: Found mainly in deciduous woodland areas, usually near water. Spends a great deal of time below the substrate, where it is an adept burrower.

CAPTIVE CARE: Requires a large woodland terrarium or an aqua-terrarium for breeding purposes. Potted plants and bark or logs under which the salamanders can hide are desirable. Maintain a high humidity and a temperature not greater than 25°C (77°F). Simulated hibernation is recommended during the winter months. Feeds on a variety of small invertebrates.

Marbled salamanders, Ambystoma opacum, *are not only attractive but they have unusual breeding habits. The eggs are laid on land.*

BREEDING: Courtship and fertilization takes place in the water after heavy rains. Females lay clumps of about 100 eggs that adhere to submersed plants.

Marbled Salamander

Ambystoma opacum
Family: Ambystomatidae
Length: 12 cm (5 in)

DESCRIPTION: Smaller than the spotted salamander but strongly built, with well-formed limbs. The ground color is black, with metallic looking, light gray hourglasses. The underside is plain black.

NATURAL RANGE: Eastern U.S.A. except for the Florida panhandle.

HABITAT AND HABITS: A variety of woodland sites. Nocturnal. More terrestrial than most *Ambystoma*.

CAPTIVE CARE: A medium sized aqua-terrarium with potted plants and hiding places. The water area need not take up more than 25% of the floor space. Summer temperatures to 25°C (77°F) are satisfactory,

reduced in winter for simulated hibernation. Feeds on a variety of small invertebrates.

BREEDING: Courtship and fertilization occur on land, after which the female lays up to 200 eggs in a damp depression in the ground. She usually curls around the eggs to protect them until the rains come to form puddles of water in which the larvae will hatch. The larvae transform into fully terrestrial forms in four to six months.

Tiger Salamander

Ambystoma tigrinum
Family: Ambystomatidae
Length: 40 cm (13½ in)

DESCRIPTION: There is a great variation in size among the many subspecies of tiger salamander, but the maximum length given above would make it the world's largest land salamander. The average length, however, is more in the region of 18 cm (8 in). It is a robust species with a broad head and relatively small eyes. The color and pattern are extremely variable. Ground color may be greenish, grayish, or brown with yellowish stripes, spots, or marbling.

NATURAL RANGE: Widespread across most of the U.S.A. from coast to coast, and extending into Mexico. Eastern populations becoming increasingly rare.

HABITAT AND HABITS: Occupies a varied habitat, from relatively arid areas to grassy plains and mountain forests. An adept burrower that is rarely seen during the daytime. Sometimes seen at night, especially after heavy rains.

CAPTIVE CARE: A large aqua-terrarium or an aquarium for neotenous specimens. Should have a fairly deep substrate to allow for burrowing and a number of potted plants. May be kept in a temperature range of 15-25°C (59-79°F), reduced to around 5°C (41°F) in winter for simulated hibernation. Feed on large invertebrates.

The very plain Jefferson salamander, Ambystoma jeffersonianum.

BREEDING: Courtship and mating occur in temporary pools, ponds, lakes, or streams in the early spring. The eggs are laid in masses attached to water plants and submerged debris. The larvae transform in four to five months. In the western part of the range tiger salamanders are often neotenous, the larvae growing to 30 cm (12 in) in length and reproducing in this condition.

Blue-spotted Salamander
Ambystoma laterale
Family: Ambystomatidae
Length: 12.5 cm (5 in)

DESCRIPTION: An attractive, slender species, with a relatively narrow snout and short legs. Bluish black above with light blue flecks and blotches. The underside is lighter, with dark blotching or flecking.

NATURAL RANGE: Throughout the Great Lakes region and to the Atlantic coast.

HABITAT AND HABITS: Found mainly in deciduous forests, where it burrows under debris near to water.

CAPTIVE CARE: Requires a small aqua-terrarium with plants and hiding places. Humidity should be high. The summer temperature should be maintained at 15–20°C (59–68°F). For simulated hibernation they should be kept at temperatures just above freezing for two to three months. Will feed on a selection of small invertebrates.

BREEDING: Mating occurs in ponds during March and April. The female lays several batches of about 15 eggs that are

The bright colors, relative hardiness, and abundance of the spotted salamander, Ambystoma maculatum, *have made it a fairly popular pet species.*

attached to submersed plants and branches. The larvae hatch in about 30 days, and these metamorphose into terrestrial forms in four to six months.

Slimy Salamander

Plethodon glutinosus
Family: Plethodontidae
Length: 20 cm (8 in)

DESCRIPTION: The family Plethodontidae (lungless or woodland salamanders) is the largest salamander family, with about 200 species in some 20 genera. All are confined to North, Central, and South America, with the exception of two European species in the genus *Hydromantes*. The slimy salamander, like other members of the family, is lungless and breathes through its thin, moist skin. It is a slender amphibian with a round body and a flattened head. The eyes are relatively large. The color is black with cream or white spots mainly concentrated along the flanks. The belly is slate blue, often mottled with white.

NATURAL RANGE: Eastern U.S.A. and into southeastern Canada.

HABITAT AND HABITS: Found in a range of habitats from near sea level to 1600 meters (5200 ft). It hides under flat rocks and rotten logs, emerging to hunt small invertebrates. It secretes a sticky substance through its skin that is very difficult to remove should it get on the hands.

CAPTIVE CARE: Provide a terrarium with gravel and leaf litter substrate, a few potted plants and moss clumps, and flat stones or slates under which the animals can hide and breed. Maintain a summer temperature not greater than 22°C (72°F), reduced to just above 0°C (32°F) for simulated hibernation.

Humidity should be high. Feeds on a selection of small invertebrates.

BREEDING: After courtship and fertilization on land, the female lays 5–35 eggs in a hollow under a stone or rotten log. There is no aquatic larval stage, and the young hatch out as miniature terrestrial editions of the adults.

Arboreal Salamander
Aneides lugubris
Family: Plethodontidae
Length: 15 cm (6 in)

DESCRIPTION: A slender species with a relatively large head. The body is gray-brown to chocolate with yellow or cream spots; the underside is creamy white. The tail is somewhat prehensile.

NATURAL RANGE: Coastal ranges of California and Baja peninsula.

HABITAT AND HABITS: An ideal species for those requiring something out of the ordinary. It is an adept climber and spends much time hunting insects in trees and bushes. Found in both deciduous and evergreen woodlands, usually in the

Although it is virtually never available, there is no reason the arboreal salamander, Aneides lugubris, *of the San Francisco Bay area could not be acclimated to the terrarium.*

neighborhood of water.

CAPTIVE CARE: Requires a tall terrarium in which large, robust plants will live, giving the salamanders an opportunity to climb. Rocks and bark can be provided in the substrate as hiding places. Maintain a high humidity and temperatures around 25°C (77°F), reduced to 15°C (59°F) for a couple of months in the winter. Full hibernation is unnecessary. It feeds on a variety of small invertebrates.

BREEDING: Mating occurs on land, and the female lays about 20 eggs in a hollow tree or a cavity among roots. The female guards the eggs, which hatch as terrestrial replicas of the adult in three to four months.

Red Salamander
Pseudotriton ruber
Family: Plethodontidae
Length: 18 cm (7 in)

DESCRIPTION: A rather dumpy species with a relatively short tail. The color is bright orange-red with a large number of scattered small black spots.

NATURAL RANGE: Eastern U.S.A. except southeastern sea board and most of Florida.

HABITAT AND HABITS: Found in very damp habitats, particularly

Undoubtedly the red salamander, Pseudotriton ruber, *is one of the most brightly colored American salamanders. It does well in the terrarium and becomes quite tame.*

around springs and seepages, to altitudes of 1500 meters (4875 ft). Terrestrial and nocturnal.

CAPTIVE CARE: Prefers a large terrarium, preferably one with a running waterfall to maintain high humidity. Use a gravel substrate and give mossy rocks as hiding places. Maintain temperatures around 20°C (68°F) in the summer and reduce them to 2–3°C (36–38°F) for simulated winter hibernation. Like other salamanders, it feeds on a variety of small invertebrates.

BREEDING: The female lays 50–100 eggs in shallow water. The larvae metamorphose in 2–2½ years.

Suggested Reading

The following books are available in your local pet shops and book shops and T.F.H. Publications, Inc., P.O. Box 427, Neptune, NJ 07753-9989.

BREEDING TERRARIUM ANIMALS
By Elke Zimmermann
ISBN 0-86622-182-4
TFH H-1078

Hard cover, 5½"; 256 pages. Illustrated with over 200 full-color and black and white photos.
Contents: Housing. Terrarium Construction. Light and Heat. Humidity and Water. Nutrition. Natural Foods. Commercially Available Foods. Breeding Food Animals. Diseases. Breeding and Rearing. Reproductive Strategies. The Terrarium Animals.

Designed primarily for amateur or professional involved with the keeping of reptiles and amphibians, this remarkably detailed and highly specific book offers a wealth of practical, easy-to-apply advice about breeding reptiles and amphibians in captivity while providing a valuable (and highly interesting) overview of the reproductive behavior patterns of herptiles.

ENCYCLOPEDIA OF REPTILES AND AMPHIBIANS
By John F. Breen
ISBN 0-87666-220-3
TFH H-935

This book is an enormous coverage of the care, collection and identification of reptiles and amphibians. Written for amateur and professional.
Contents: Turtles Common And Rare. Other Turtles And The Tortoises. Alligators, Caimans, And Crocodiles. Native American Lizards. Exotic Lizards And The Tuatara. Harmless North American Snakes. Non-Poisonous Exotic Snakes. Poisonous Snakes. Newts, Salamanders And Caecilians. Frogs And Toads. Collecting Herptiles. Feeding A Collection. Illnesses And Other Problems.
Hard cover, 5½ x 8", 576 pages
316 black and white photos, 267 color photos.

AXOLOTLS
By Peter W. Scott
ISBN 0-87666-937-2
TFH KW-132
43 full-color photos, 41 black and white photos. Hard cover; 64 pages.

Index

Page numbers set in bold type refer to illustrations

SALAMANDERS and NEWTS
CO-043S

A young Triturus cristatus *ready for its next meal of tubifex worms.*